The Homes of Oberammergau

The Homes of Oberammergau

by Eliza Greatorex

edited, with an introduction, by Gordon Mork

afterword by Otto Huber

NotaBell Books
An imprint of Purdue University Press
West Lafayette, Indiana

Contents

Introduction

In 1871 Eliza Greatorex, an American widow with three children, spent a summer in Oberammergau. Drawn by the stories she knew of the famous Passion Play and searching for fitting subjects for her artistic activity, she reached the Bavarian village in a horse-drawn coach. Her journal and its illustrations are both charming and insightful. The traveler of the twenty-first century will recognize many of the same elements that Greatorex did in the nineteenth century. While much has changed in Oberammergau and the world beyond, there are also continuities which deserve our attention.

Eliza Pratt was born on Christmas day 1819 in Manor Hamilton, Ireland. Her father was a Wesleyan preacher who moved the family to New York City when she was twenty-one. Both she and her sister Matilda were encouraged to develop their talents as artists and writers, and Matilda eventually wrote a novel based on their childhood, *Kilrogan Cottage*.[1] In New York Eliza began to develop her skills as a painter and illustrator.

When Eliza was thirty she married Henry Wellington Greatorex, a relatively well-known composer of church music who was sought after as an organist. His father, Thomas Greatorex, had been organist in Westminster Abbey in London. Henry Greatorex's hymn tune, "Praise God from Whom All Blessings Flow," is familiar in many Protestant churches yet today. In addition to his religious music, he also wrote some popular secular music. Eliza wrote the words for one of his songs, "Love me forever though my cheek paleth fast."

They had three children, Kathleen Honora, Eleanor Elizabeth, and Thomas Walter. The family traveled widely, in England,
Ireland, and America, as Henry Greatorex performed concerts and
had teaching engagements. He died unexpectedly in 1858 just after
returning from England. Eliza was only thirty-nine and left with
the three children under eight years old. She settled in New York
and opened an artist's studio on Broadway. There she supported
herself and her young family by teaching at a girls' school, giving
private lessons, and selling her own work. All the time she continued
her own studies, working with William H. Witherspoon and James
Hart, and she looked for new opportunities to develop her talents.

In 1861 she traveled to Paris to study with a French land-
scapist, Emile Lambinet, and soon reached out to Germany and
Italy as well for new sources of inspiration. She was able to gain
financial success by publishing her work as etchings. Back in New
York she became the only female member of the Artist Fund Society during the 1860s, and in 1869 she was one of the few women
elected an associate member of the National Academy of Art.[2]

She traveled to Germany in 1870, settling first on Nuremberg as a place to create romantic views of the past, and these etchings were published in 1875. During the winter of 1870–71 the family
lived in Munich, where she studied art and copied the old masters
at the great Pinakothek museum. In the summer of 1871 she went
on to Oberammergau. The passion play had been scheduled for
the summer of 1870, but it had been interrupted by the outbreak
of the Franco-Prussian War.

When Eliza arrived in Oberammergau in the summer of
1871, the war with France had just been concluded, and Germany
was now united under Bismarck's leadership. The returning troops,
therefore, had a double reason to celebrate: victory over the French
and unity as a powerful state. But Eliza had little sympathy for
such blatant nationalism. She hoped for a more pure and pacific
vision as she set off for the fabled village of the passion play, first
by train, then by horse-drawn coach, and finally on foot.

At this time the Oberammergau tradition was already over
two centuries old. In 1634 the Oberammergau Passion Play was

first performed in the midst of the Thirty Years' War. In the year 1633 there were only a few score families in the village, and its isolation in the Bavarian Alps spared it from the worst of the war itself. But the war brought pestilence, and suddenly Oberammergau found itself in the grip of an epidemic that threatened to devastate every household. In desperation the people turned to God. It was a solidly Roman Catholic village, so the town fathers gathered around the crucifix at the parish church and took a pledge. If God would preserve the village from this dreadful plague, they promised that they would perform a play based on Christ's suffering, death, and resurrection once every ten years forever. According to local tradition, no one else in Oberammergau died of the plague from that day on. The next year, 1634, the first performance was given in the village, by and for the villagers themselves.

Passion plays, like the medieval mystery plays and the many festivals of piety to which they are closely related, were once very popular throughout Europe. So there were texts available for the villagers to learn, and priests and schoolmasters to give them guidance. Two monasteries were nearby: the Augustinians at Rottenbuch and the Benedictines at Ettal. Over the decades old texts were revised and new ones written. Beginning in 1680, the town began to give the play in every zero-numbered year, and the tradition took hold. The Oberammergau Passion Play was a religious obligation, an artistic performance, and a local festival; by the nineteenth century it had become a famous tradition.[3]

Eliza Pratt Greatorex's description of her summer in Oberammergau can be appreciated on several levels. First and foremost it provides a verbal picture of village, the villagers, and the sometimes outrageously rude visitors to accompany the lovely sketches, which give her book its name. Included in her narrative are entries from the notebooks of her two teenaged daughters, who were apprentice artists and writers learning the craft under their mother's tutelage.

Secondly, it provides a commentary by an American woman, a self-sufficient single mother, and a Protestant in a deeply

Catholic region. She shows genuine affection for the people she comes to know, but she is critical of their society as well. She sees the women of Oberammergau in particular, and of Germany in general, patiently bearing the weight of a patriarchal system. Yet she emphasizes the simple piety and good cheer of the villagers. Through her eyes we can see the players of the sacred drama in their everyday lives, including the joys and sorrows of life and death in the village as they presented their passion play for some 30,000 visitors that summer.

Thirdly, we get glimpses of the aspects of the Oberammergau Passion Play that became controversial after the Holocaust. The play that Eliza saw was a melodrama of "good Christians" versus "bad Jews," and Judas was portrayed as the greatest villain of the piece. This was the text of the play that Adolf Hitler saw twice, in 1930 and 1934, and which he and other Nazis praised as "anti-Semitic." Calls for reform were increasingly heard, both from within the village and in the greater world, after World War II. The Roman Catholic Church made important doctrinal reforms in the 1960s, recognizing that it was wrong to blame "the Jews" for the suffering and death of Jesus. Reforms were introduced into the Oberammergau Passion Play, haltingly at first, and more strongly in the 1990 version under the direction of Christian Stückl and Otto Huber. The production of 2000, while still using most of the basic text seen by Eliza in 1871, has eliminated the offensively anti-Jewish portions and recognized the essential Jewishness of Jesus.[4]

Finally, the book is sufficiently introspective to give us a view of the artist and writer herself, and indeed of her daughters. We can see her constructing a romantic vision of the village that was not immediately apparent to the visitor. This vision was created by the artist herself from the raw material she found in the Bavarian Alps and put together into an attractive package for those who might read her words and enjoy her pictures. She was initially disappointed when she saw the town, but once she got to know it better, she realized that she had attractive material for her artistic expression. She would set up her easel in various places,

seeking the best angles and the best light, all the while exercising her rudimentary German to get to know the people.

After Oberammergau Eliza returned to New York, where she received a commission to go to Colorado and prepare etchings of the mountain scenery, which were published in 1873. Back in New York, she began to develop various artistic items coming into demand as the United States approached its centennial year. Her etching set *Old New York, From the Battery to Bloomingdale*, with a text by her sister, Matilda Pratt Despard, was a success. And she combined a commercial sense with artistic talent to create a range of decorative items—on china, wood, and architectural fragments—to celebrate the country's birthday in 1876. In 1879 she went to Paris to study etching with Charles Henri Toussaint. Her work has been compared favorably with that of Mary Cassatt, who worked in Paris at the same time, though there is apparently no evidence that they knew one another. One of her etchings of the French countryside was published by the *American Art Review* in 1881.[5]

She continued to work closely with her two daughters, and the three of them traveled in England, Germany, Italy, and Algiers before returning to New York in 1881. Her work was shown in the Paris Salon, the New York Etching Club, the Boston Museum of Fine Arts, and at other prestigious venues, as well as being published in various forms. After her son, Thomas, died in Colorado in 1881, her daughters moved with her back to Paris in 1886, from which they continued to travel and produce items of artistic value. She died in 1897, as did her daughter Eleanor. Kathleen continued to work as an artist till her death in 1913.

In an afterward following Eliza's account, Otto Huber gives us the reflections of a man who has grown up with the passion play as a native of the twentieth-century village. He first appeared in the passion play as a child in 1950, along with his grandfather, who played Peter. In the year 1990, and again in the year 2000, he has had a vital role in forming and executing the current version of the Oberammergau tradition, as the deputy director, author, and

dramaturge, and by playing the role of the prologue speaker. The passion play cannot be a museum piece, he believes, and his essay looks both to the historical past, as presented by Eliza and her daughters, and to the future.

Notes

1.   New York: Harper and Brothers, 1878.

2.   *Appletons' Cyclopaedia of American Biography* (New York, 1900). April F. Masten in the *American National Biography* (New York: Oxford University Press, 1999) 9:464–65, and Phyllis Peet, *American Women of the Etching Revival* (Atlanta, Ga.: High Museum of Art, 1988), 57–58.

3.   The literature on the Passion Play at Oberammergau is rich and colorful, and the best place to start is the publications of the Oberammergauers themselves. See the volumes published regularly in each play year, like *Passion Oberammergau 1990* (Oberammergau, 1990), richly illustrated, and with a commentary by Otto Huber (in both German and English) and *Hört, sehet, weint und liebt: Passionsspiele im alpenländischen Raum* (Munich: Haus der bayerischen Geschichte, 1990).

4.   The list of critical literature is long, including a bitter but well-documented account by an American, Saul S. Friedman, *The Oberammergau Passion Play: A Lance against Civilization* (Carbondale, Ill.: Southern Illinois University Press, 1984). For a summary of the successful reforms through 1990, see Gordon R. Mork, "'Wicked Jews' and 'Suffering Christians' in the Oberammergau Passion Play," in *Representations of Jews through the Ages*, edited by Leonard Jay Greenspoon and Bryan F. Le Beau (Omaha, Nebr.: Creighton University Press, 1996), 153–69.

5.   S. R. Koehler, "The Works of the American Etchers: XXII.— Mrs. Eliza Greatorex," *American Art Review* 2, part 2 (1881): 12.

GOING INTO OBERAMMERGAU

THE HOMES

OF

OBER-AMMERGAU.

A SERIES OF
TWENTY ETCHINGS
IN HELIOTYPE, FROM THE ORIGINAL PEN-
AND-INK DRAWINGS,
TOGETHER WITH
NOTES FROM A DIARY
KEPT DURING A THREE MONTHS' RESIDENCE
IN OBER-AMMERGAU, IN THE SUMMER OF 1871,

BY
ELIZA GREATOREX.

MUNICH:
PUBLISHED BY JOS. ALBERT,
PHOTOGRAPHER TO THE COURTS OF MUNICH AND ST. PETERSBURG.
1872.

F. STRAUB, PRINTER TO THE ROYAL ACADEMY OF SCIENCES,

MUNICH, BAVARIA.

DEDICATED
TO THE
GEISTLICHER RATH
DAISENBERGER.

Wishing to associate my work with the hearts as well as the homes of Ober-Ammergau, I ask permission to dedicate it to you, dear Pastor, who, by your great learning, constant self-sacrifice, and the deep piety of a loving and gentle heart, have guided the people whose homes I have here portrayed, during so many years of your long and successful ministry, towards that Christ-life whose story they so wonderfully personate.

EVENING: THROUGH THE TREES

I.

THE JOURNEY TO THE PASSION PLAY.

I have promised the children that I will write something for them every day while we are separated. We have been close together ever since we left home in New York, a year and three months ago. Now I have left them standing on the platform at Munich, somewhat disconsolate, the words "I wish you would not go, mother! Do stay with us to see the return of the Bavarian troops!" ringing in my ears up to the last moment. But, leaving them in good care, I am starting off for something that I am glad to be able to see alone—the Passion Play at Oberammergau. To be sure, my eyes are a little moist, but I console myself with the thought that, if this is a thing pure and good, that I can accept for myself and them, it will be charming to write to them about it, and to bring them to see it also, after all this excitement attendant on the coming home of the troops to Munich, —so sad, so desolate the city all winter, but now half buried under flags and rich adornments, and deeply stirred, too, with emotion on the return of the few out of the many brave men who went out just this time last year.*

* The Franco-Prussian War began in July 1870, after a diplomatic clash engineered by Otto von Bismarck. Bavaria was still an independent state at that time, but in the outburst of anti-French patriotism, soon joined with Prussia in the attack on France. During the war, negotiations among the German states created the new German Empire. So the returning Bavarians were celebrating both the victory over France and the unification of Germany. The 1870 passion play season was interrupted after seventeen performances. The 1871 resumption had eighteen performances.

We were in old Nuremberg then; and while I see the groups of
these returning ones by the side of the track, where they have been
encamped all night, looking so happy and at rest, and making themselves every inch bright and clean, in order to take part in the festal
entry into the gay capital, I cannot but think of the time when
that sudden war-storm swept over Germany, giving them hardly a
moment of time for partings from mothers and sweethearts, wives
and children, under the shadows of old courtways and walls of long
ago. The whole war was to me too terrible. If it is true that in yon
mountain village the people are worthy to represent scenes from
the Divine life of Christ, the Prince of Peace, and with simple and
devout hearts to make it their chief religious service, I shall count
it but small loss to have missed seeing the glittering pageantry connected with the welcoming home of the victorious soldiers.

July 14, 1871. — The grey morning and the level plain are bright
with peasants in costume, trudging towards Munich, through fields
of potatoe-blossom and rich spreads of corn with garniture of
glowing poppies and blue corn-flower. From a copse close by, a
troop of cavalry rides out. How bright, how inspiring, everything
is! I feel strangely happy, although you young people are left behind. Here is lovely Starnberg, with the smiling lake, of which we
catch heavenly peeps between the trees, as we pass along the shores
of the green water to Weilheim. But what a crowding and fuss, a
rush for seats and omnibus there is when we get there! I am to sit
in the coupé of the post-diligence,* and I give a little shiver, indeed, as I realize that I am all alone, without you children to help
me out with my German; but speak I must to the postman who
sits beside me, and as we pass the pretty villages dotting the plain
I venture to ask him questions in quantities, and get along much
better than I had anticipated. We approach Murnau, towards the

* A stage coach run by the postal service. Note the coaches climbing the
steep road to the monastery town of Ettal in "Going into Oberammergau,"
p. 7. The railroad did not reach Oberammergau until the 1900 play year.

THE HOUSE OF THE ZWINKS ("Matthew" & "John")

glorious mountains, shining in the sunlight far away. As we come closer, what a delicious valley is here! O, happy people, do you know what a joy you have, or is it because I have not seen for four long summers mountain sides sloping down to deep green valleys, thick beds of blossom and little winding streams, where the rushes grow thick, that I feel mine to be so great? At Oberau a cup of coffee fought for and enjoyed, more confusion, baggage lost or left, and the start to walk up the great steep hill of Ettal, beyond which lie the valley of the Ammer and the village of Oberammergau. As we stop to rest here and there, I find many pleasant people to talk to, English, Scotch and Irish, though I think all the Americans must have remained in Munich, to see the festivities. There is certainly a happy spirit in this mountain region! The scenery reminds me of many a climb I have had among the Catskills, back of our dear old Hudson River at home. My heart warms to God's sunny world and His loving ones in it. From the bright bit of blue we catch above us, down to the mysteries of the deep ravine on our left, where the waters leap and sing, my eyes find deep delight, nature wraps my whole being in a blessed rest, and how much I want you with me to share it. It has been a huge climb.

But here we are at the top, breathing purer air than ever. In a few minutes we are in Ettal. I am conscious of a splendid pile of buildings, of a great old dome, but my eyes are straining for the village of Oberammergau. Now we are beside the Ammer, and seemingly quite near us, on our left, rises the curiously peaked Kofel,* the sunlight falling on the high cross that the people of Ammergau have planted on its summit. In a little turn of the road, on our right, is a rocky cavern, where we must stop a minute, as we get our first peep of the village church, with the grey and red-roofed cottages of the village nestling around it. I know there must be lovely points of view about here; but we have only a moment, to peer into the cave in the crag above us, where we can dimly discern a

---

* Kofel is the name of the mountain peak which rises sharply over the town and is surmounted by a huge cross. Oberammergau is 840 meters above sea level, and the Kofel is 1,342 meters above sea level.

crucifix and shrine, up to which there is a well-worn foot-path, and lower down is another shrine with the Madonna and Child in a frame of little round holy pictures, and scribbled all over with the names of ambitious travellers. Even the Madonna's face is not spared! What a pity it is that in Bavaria the people associate sacred things with forms that must shock every sense of the beautiful! One can but turn away and think it is their best and they believe that they do right. I hear most musical bells, and from one mountain side come the cows of the village, while from the other, across the river, a goat-herd boy drives home his flock, and we go in with them, to find our resting places, while the sun sets red behind the long straight street, closed to our view by the church, with its large cross lifted high above the crowd of lesser ones marking the houses so strongly. Yet I have no pleasure, as I stand at last in full sight of Oberammergau. All is cold, and stiff, and straight; and I give a great sigh of disappointment as I acknowledge that there is nothing picturesque! But the door of Flunger's house, one of the first in the street, opens of itself, and I find comfort after my day's journey.

There seems to be a large family of the Flungers, though I have spoken only to one young woman, who has been helping me to find my luggage, which went on to the post. As I go through the village, I feel more hopeful, though it is the oddest place I have ever seen, the street by which one enters giving no idea of what lies beyond. As we come back to the Flunger house, and while I am standing in the gateway that leads into a shady garden, I am introduced to a young countryman of mine, who has been staying some weeks in the house. I am told that there are very few strangers in the village; but I have seen three English ladies by the river side, just opposite the priest's house, painting in water colors, and making me wish that I, too, could express myself in that way, for it seems so easy in it to do good things rapidly. We have dinner in the garden. I say we; for my countryman is very pleasant, and has been here so long that I am happy to talk with him about the place and the people; and he is very enthusiastic about both. The young woman, Franziska, and her younger sister Josepha, —Francie and

Sefie, as they are called for short here, —pass in and out of the
garden, carrying into the kitchen large tubs of water on a pole between them, from the fountain close by the roadside. I look at their
fresh and winning faces, as they bring out our dinner, —which is
simple, but most eatable, in this delightful shade of linden trees,
with sweet odors coming to us from the little flower beds in front
of the house, and from the young hop vines stretching up long
poles, —and I hear that the elder girl, this simple, sweet-faced
maiden of twenty-six years, is the Virgin Mary of the Passion Play.
I admire, too, her sister Sefie, who, with her dark brown hair done
up tightly, and clad in short grey petticoat and coarse white linen
bodice, goes about in her blue stockings and strong black slippers,
carrying with her everywhere a bright and most winning smile. But
her shapely hands are worn with hard work, and as I look from
her to some of the older women around, and note the fearful
change that toil more than age must bring to these two comely
girls, I cannot bear to think of it, and wish with all my heart, that
they were in a country such as my own dear one, where men do
not sit still while women's shoulders strain, and their backs bend
as these do here.*

I write this in the garden, though now it is after six o'clock
supper. The great heat is past, and we have watched the people
coming in for the festival, some of them to this house. Two students from Oxford occupy the large guest-chamber, and we have a
literary lady from Florence, who travelled here alone all night in a
carriage from Innsbruck. As we sit and see the visitors coming freely
to the family, and observe with what kindness they are made welcome, it does seem an out of the world place. The girls are now
talking with ladies and gentlemen, and in honor of them wear
dresses. How much better they looked in their costume! Some
Americans come in, and make presents of money, a little publicly,
and I am somewhat annoyed about it, for it cannot be a good thing

---

* American feminists might be surprised at this favorable comparison.
We must remember that Eliza Greatorex was able to make a good living
for herself and her children as an artist and illustrator.

to do. But here comes the village band, and as it starts from the front of our garden we stand up, and join the throng. First come the firemen, then the musicians, and now they parade through the streets, to the Passion Theatre. What a lovely view!

July 16. — I have just had my first night of country air and bed in Bavarian Tyrol. I found everything clean and sweet. I have a plumeau,* certainly, but also a fresh red flannel blanket, on which Sefie herself must have sewn the pure white linen sheet. Declining coffee in my own room, I go down to the family, and find three sisters and the mother in the kitchen. It is pleasant to hear their gay "Good mornings," to take from Francie my bowl of coffee, and carry it myself into the little "living room," where I am met by Tobias Flunger, with a dignified, but most friendly greeting. I will put myself and my coffee into the corner, with my back to the stove, and dare to look at this man, who is said to have made in 1850 the most beautiful "Christus" ever seen in Ammergau. Now he appears a man grave and self-possessed, of a most interesting countenance, a little pre-occupied, but ready with a pleasant smile to answer my broken sentences, and to help me out in the effort of expression. He is plaiting a crown of thorns for the "Christus" of to-morrow, cutting off those that might hurt, and as I watch him at his strange work, I ask myself, what is this I am to see?

---

* A featherbed.

THE VILLAGE: THROUGH THE TREES

II.

SETTLING IN THE VILLAGE

July 16. — Dear children! We must give up all idea of our projected summer sojourn at Berchtesgaden,* and you must come up
here to me at once. I cannot write about what I have seen and felt
to-day; but I have decided to live among these people, if possible,
this summer, and see how their daily life accords with this marvel-
lous religious service. Remember, we must live with the people, in
order to do this; and I know you well enough to be sure that you
will not grumble about the boiled beef, which will, no doubt, be
frequent. There will be many little discomforts, but also much else
to make these seem very small. To-morrow I begin to sketch, for I
have found many picturesque old houses; and the church, the Kofel
and the Ammer, together, give the village a character peculiarly its
own. We are to stay at the house of the Flungers, where I have
taken rooms for the summer. They are all so good and kind, and are
always talking of when you children will come and join the house.
But now to my pleasant work. Monday morning: It is but half past
six, as I settle myself to work, in a bower made by the tops of beech
and fir trees and young poplars, that stretch up to and shade the high
entrance to the theatre. I have tied back the boughs, that I may the
better see my picture, which is a gay one. The sun is making fire-
works round the tall church spire and the roofs of the houses that

---

* Sixty years later, Berchtesgaden would become the summer retreat of
Adolf Hitler. Hitler was born in 1889 in the town of Braunau, along the
Austrian-Bavarian border.

cluster about it. Every moment gives fresh colour to the distant hills, and the Kofel is wide awake atop, and smiles down at the mists as they creep up his wooded sides. The coffee was made long ago, and men, women and children are at work in the fields. Very different was last evening, when, the great Drama over, the crowd gone, I stood here all alone, and thought of the living pictures those peasants, now making hay down there in the meadows, had painted on my inmost heart during that long day of strange emotion. And while I silently prayed that the great act of devotion in which I had shared might bring me nearer to the Christ-life, the village looked in the soft twilight of the lovely valley, a place wherein to rest and to live a better, happier life.

Friday Evening. — On my way down to Ettal to meet you, I stop under the crag where the shrines are, and where one gets the first glimpse of the village. I have been thinking over the four days since I last wrote to you, and my first note is, that my great drawing that was to have been taken from the high entrance to the theatre, is a failure, and that I must not be so ambitious in future. My next note is, that although the people grow more into my heart each day I am with them, and although the garden is sweeter than ever, there is a painful feeling of something wrong creeping in. But this may be only my own foolish fears, or else it may be my bad drawing that is on my mind. There are more wild flowers than I ever saw before. It seems as if Nature had emptied her whole harmony of colour over road-side and meadow, beside this sweet river bank, and I only want your fresh young faces, to tune my spirits to the song of birds and to the laughter of the flowers and the ferns, that looking down into the clear waters, find out how beautiful they are.

  I sit now in the church of Ettal with the children. There are moments in life that compensate for days of loss! We are listening to the grand old organ,* played by the under-teacher from

* Eliza's husband, Henry Greatorex, was a fine church organisr. He had died in 1858.

Oberammergau. Crowds of peasants make the tour of the beautiful little church, with its saintly skeletons in glass cases, gorgeously arrayed, and pictures painted by Knoller* hanging above them. The peasants press close to the great treasure of the church, the Ettal Madonna, eager to kiss her hands, feet and face and the infant Jesus in her arms. There is a legend of this Madonna which I have found. The Emperor of Germany, Ludwig the Bavarian,† went in the year 1327 with his army to Italy, to restore order there, and to be crowned in Rome as the German or Holy Roman Emperor. But after he was crowned, Robert, the King of Naples, threatened to cut off his retreat; and he therefore made haste to retire to Germany. The Italians were never very well satisfied with the German dominion, and soon other forces joined those of Robert's; and when Ludwig reached Milan, that city closed its gates against him, too. This was in the year 1329. Ludwig was in great distress, not knowing where to get assistance, or money wherewith to pay his men, when a remarkable event, so the story tells us, aided in his deliverance out of the difficulty. One day he entered the little chapel of the monastery of St. Victor, where he was staying, and while praying to the Virgin for aid, an aged monk appeared before him (some accounts say it was an angel), and gave him a small image of the Madonna, telling him, that if he would make a vow to build a monastery for Benedictine monks in the Valley of the Ammer, and place in it the image of the Madonna for public veneration as soon as he reached Bavaria, he would return home without further difficulty.

Ludwig promised this, and money coming into his treasury, he was enabled to pay his troops; and shortly afterwards he left Italy, and began his march homewards. The Emperor did not forget his vow, and when he arrived at Partenkirchen, he asked to

---

* Martin Knoller, 1725–1804, was a Tyrolian rococo painter.

† Ludwig IV, the Bavarian, was Holy Roman Emperor from 1314 to 1347. He was the only Bavarian to be elected Holy Roman Emperor. Like many other medieval emperors, he was engaged in a serious struggle with the papacy.

THE HOUSE OF GREGOR STADLER ("Annas")

be guided to this lovely valley of the Ammer; when another miraculous event determined the monarch in the selection of the place whereon to erect the monastery. After riding up the dreadfully steep hill of Ettal, bearing the image in his arms, he was astonished to find his horse fall upon its knees three times; and the Emperor took this event as a hint from heaven that here he should carry his vow into execution. Wicked people assert that the horse was exhausted with bearing its master up the hill, and fell down on its knees because it could not go any further. I well remember how the limbs of our poor animal trembled the other day, in merely drawing a light empty chaise up the hill! But Ludwig had great faith, and in the year 1330 he laid the foundation stone of the convent and church, and made the institution a kind of asylum for aged knights, and a residence for Benedictine monks, the latter of whom remained in Ettal until the great secularization in 1803.*

Many a hard time has the Ettal Madonna passed through, and many a miraculous escape, too. The convent was repeatedly plundered by hostile soldiers, but the Madonna always escaped, with at most a few bruises. In the year 1703, when war raged in these mountains, the image was sent to Munich for preservation in one of the churches there, but it was soon brought back again to Ettal in triumph, borne on a gayly decorated wagon, accompanied by immense crowds of people, the clergy and nobles. Its reputation as possessing miraculous virtues is wide-spread, and even to this day processions of pilgrims come, mostly from Suabia,† to pay their devotions to it, though not in anything like the numbers that formerly came. Two centuries ago as many as seventy thousand pilgrims are said to have visited Ettal in the course of a single year! The peculiar virtues of the image are said to consist in its being "to the pure-minded as light as a feather, to the impure and

---

* At the end of the Holy Roman Empire, during the Napoleonic Wars, most monastery lands were taken from the church, and monsteries themselves were closed. Benedictine monks returned to Ettal in the twentieth century, when the buidings were reopened as a school.

† Swabia, in the neighboring state of Württemberg.

haughty weighing a hundred pounds, but quite invisible to the guilty." The pilgrims earlier believed that the stone from which the image is made came directly from heaven, and that the figure had proportions more beautiful than could be made by mortal hands; but art historians have proved that the image is an excellent work from the school of Andrea of Pisano (who died in 1345), who worked under the immediate influence of Giotto.* The villagers of Ammergau perform at times a very interesting drama entitled, "the Founding of the monastery of Ettal," in which the whole legendary story of the Madonna is embodied. It was written by the Geistlicher Rath Daisenberger,† who was for many years priest of the village, and who still lives at Oberammergau, in the enjoyment of all his faculties, doing all he can to promote the interests of his people whom he loves, and their great play.

The church at Ettal is rococo, of the most decorative description. The under-teacher led us into the sacristy, where the old furniture of the church, dating from the fourteenth century, is kept. There are beautifully inlaid cabinets, containing some old vestments, and a very few relics, for this monastery, once so rich and full of art treasures, has but little left. Only yesterday Flunger showed me a large portfolio full of engravings of Albrecht Durer's,‡ that had come from the monastery years ago. We certainly saw little of art, as we passed with the crowd into a long vaulted chamber, one end nearly filled up by an immense stove, curious paintings, proverbs and inscriptions, with maps darkened by age, hanging on the walls. All around the sides of the room were ranged narrow beds, and at one end were tables for the overplus of guests, who

---

* Giotto di Bondone, 1267–1337, was an Italian painter.

† "Geistlicher Rat" means "spiritual counselor" and is used here as a term of special respect. Father Daisenberger was the chief author of the play text used in 1871 and (with important revisions) still used today. Eliza Greatorex dedicated her book to him.

‡ Albrecht Dürer, 1471–1528, was a German artist. Note that the humble villagers of Oberammergau were well acquainted with great works of Western art, and their passion play reflected this sophistication.

were busily disposing of the black bread, cheese and beer. Hungry and thirsty peasants they were, smoking, laughing and talking on every side. Now on our way home, we stand, just within the entrance arch, arrested by the wondrous effect of light, just at this moment flashing over the mountain beyond. It has been a day of soft cloud and sunshine mingled, and now the sun's rays have caught the light mists, and for a moment one can believe that some bright spirit has stayed his heavenward steps, to bless and glorify the landscape. Of the lovely walk home, the warm welcome of the Flunger family, who came to meet us, the delight of my young people in every body, and everything, and the great "fixing up" of our two rooms to the best advantage, it would take much time to tell. Now we sit in the garden; and watch the gathering of the band just opposite, —a handsome manly group, as I see them through our hop vines, the ever-helping Kofel in the background, and the sturdy peasants crushing down our currant bushes near by.

Extract from Nora's* Note Book. — Sunday Morning, July 23. Awoke this morning to hear canon and their echoes among the mountains. We had hardly left the garden last night before down came the unwelcome rain; and now the poor people going to this "living picture gathering," as mother calls it, trudge through the thick mud. We have not been able to get seats for to day's performance. The band is just starting. It is hard to keep from going, too. When all is quiet below we go down for our coffee. A sudden hush comes upon everything. Here in the living-room are the Flungers, the father, son and two young girls. The father is very attractive, and his manner is full of dignity. He has now taken down an old violin from its peg near the door, and tells me he has taken part in the Passion Play ever since 1820, when he was a child, and stood in the tableaux. In 1830 he sang in the chorus; in 1840 he

---

* Nora is Kathleen Honora Greatorex, 1851–1913, who became a well-known artist in her own right. At this point, she was twenty years old. The other two children were Eleanor Elizabeth (Nellie), 1854–1897, and Walter.

WASHDAY UNDER THE KOFEL

played in the orchestra, on the violin now in his hands; in 1850 he was the "Christus"; and in 1860, 1870 and 1871 the "Pilatus." A fine crayon portrait of him hangs on the wall. It is a little sad to look at it, so very beautiful and Christ-like, and then at the real man, so grey and worn.

Sefie, who is one of the Guardian Angels, looks very modest, and blushes a little as I wonder at the change I see in her; for last evening her hair was all tightly coiled round her pretty head; to-day it is in curls, falling down to her waist. Franzisca, the "Mary," is quietly getting our coffee, and attending to our comfort. The son, who plays in the orchestra, is rushing around for neck-tie and collar, evidently afraid of being too late. We go to the gate with them, the girls each carrying a basket with dinner for their father and some of the guests who will not come home at the "pause." It is very strange to see them so quiet and steady going, when they have such wonderful things to do before so great an audience, but Mother says that is the reason why the Sacred Drama is so beautifully given by them. They bring to it working hands held out in love, pious hearts lifted up in faith to their Divine Lord; and with their lowly peasant life has mingled the dignity of the life of Christ, whose story they have been born for generations to tell, until their common human nature has become, during the Passion-Time at least, strangely touched by the feeling of a Sublime Presence. I cannot yet understand this myself, but I write it down, hoping that I may do so after we have been in what I hardly like to call a theatre, since mother has told me how her soul worshipped, while these peasants represented the sufferings and sacrifice of Christ.

THE VALLEY OF THE AMMER

III.

FIRST WEEK OF VILLAGE LIFE.

July 25. — A rainy day! And since it is impossible to get to our work in the open air, we amuse ourselves, as well as we can, in exploring our home. Francie and Sefie are determined to make our sojourn in their house as agreeable as possible, and invite us to look over the family treasures of the large Guest Chamber. It is a room full of all sorts of curiosities. In one corner, is a large bookcase, curtained off with chintz, on the top of which are arranged wood-carvings, in all stages of progress, figures of Scripture characters, and, what is Flunger's special work, carved deer, in all positions, and of all sizes. Next in order comes the grand wardrobe of the family, and this being a rainy day, Frau Flunger gives permission for us to see its treasures, which Francie and Sefie show us with great pride. They begin with the gala dresses of the mother in her younger days, when she was the prettiest girl in all the country around, as her husband was the handsomest of the men. There were bodices of salmon-color, embroidered with rich flowers of all shades, and light blue ones with silver trimmings; there were handsome shawls, and silk brocaded handkerchiefs, of every hue; but the great gems of the collection were the long silver chains, which fastened the bodices cross-wise, and were held by large silver hooks. There were rosaries of silver filigree, with rich beads; one, very costly, had a turquois, which they prized much. These had belonged to their great-grandmother. As each article was exhibited, we were told to which member of the family it was to descend. I should like to see these maidens dressed in some of

this finery, but I think that comes rarely to pass. After the wardrobe came the glass cupboard, with the birthday presents of china, groups of figures, shell ornaments, and flowers.

Next morning is fine, and we get out to the church. The music is even better than in the theatre. A good orchestra, composed of several violins and three violincellos, with a good number of wind instruments, well played, and the voices not being strained, as when singing in the open air, went charmingly in unison. The leader is the schoolmaster, who directs all the village music, and selects well that which is performed at church. The older priest is a most venerable looking man. The Catholic spirit is over and in all the service. It must be a proud heart, however, that cannot consent to worship here, among the happy, honest and most devout looking congregation.* Both the aged and the younger priest seem to be a part of their people, and of their church. There are no ladies painting by the priest's house, for a wonder! It begins to rain again, so we give up hope of work, and go home to our great room to dinner, and then for a long walk in the grey afternoon, with Sefie. Returning, I sit down in the family room, and chat with the elder people. I find that Flunger studied art for some years in the Munich Academy under Konrad Eberhard,† the sculptor, but the great life of the city did not suit him; he returned to his native village, fell in love, married, and took the position of drawing master in the village. A story is told that once, in later times, Eberhard visited the Passion Play, and seeing his former scholar, embraced him, and deeply moved, said that he had never had a scholar who had given him so much true pleasure as Flunger, by his part in the Passionsspiel. That, he said, was Art in the service of God! Flunger still likes to talk about that time at the Academy, and remembers his old teacher with great love.

---

* Eliza and her children were firmly Protestant, having grown up in the spirit of the Methodist Church and the Church of England. Her comments on the Catholic spirit of the village, and yet her perception of its tolerance, are notable.

† Konrad Eberhard, 1768–1859, was a Bavarian sculptor and painter.

Another day of rain, but the girls come and say that our neighbor Hans will bring his zither, and play us some dance music in the evening; when we have much pleasure. Nora, Nellie and Walter, with Francie, Malie (an elder sister), and Frau Karl, have a gay dance, to the pretty music made by the hard, red fingers of Hans. Frau Karl and Malie dance the peasant dance with much spirit. It was hard work for Hans, but to encourage him he had a mighty mug of beer at his elbow. Frau Karl sang some merry Tyrolese airs, with the "jodel," and Francie and Sefie sang the "Edelweiss." I find nothing out of keeping in their mirth, certainly nothing to shock one's sense of propriety; but there is a simplicity of home life and harmony through it all. In the morning we must leave our big room to be scrubbed, and set thoroughly to rights for the company, which may be here on Friday. It still rains hard, and a crowd is expected this time, as it is the height of the season. Every seat in the theatre is taken, and our house will, I fear be too full to be pleasant; but we have found a retreat in the atelier of the village school, where, by permission of Flunger, I can plant my easel, and we can all study or read in quiet. It is very late when the expected guests arrive, and in what a torrent of rain! Drenched and forlorn, they must be this wild summer's night. I hear sounds quite unlike the usual friendly greetings. Several people have arrived, and soon Sefie runs up to tell us all about the difficulty. A foreign lady, with two pet poodles, and her husband, had just arrived in a carriage, and all were quite wet through. They were immediately shown upstairs, and into the large guest chamber, where two snow-white beds had been made ready for them. The lady was very solicitous about the health of the dogs, and made a great deal of fuss about her fears that the little brutes would take cold from their exposure; and drenched as they were, she insisted in placing them between the clean sheets of one of the beds, to the horror of the good Frau Flunger, who became very much exasperated at this insult to her sense of household cleanliness, and ordered the dogs to be turned unceremoniously out of the bed. Fortunately, matters were set to rights, by the dogs having couches prepared for their reception.

Now begins our first week of work, for the wet weather is happily over. This busy Saturday morning, the village is alive

and full of strangers, and seems another place since yesterday. I
meet few of my own people, as I pass through the crowded, noisy
street to my place by the house of Joseph Mayer.* I need all this
fresh morning light and hope for my subject, hard and square, and
utterly unpicturesque in itself. I have looked round everywhere for
its best point, and now sheltered from the people by empty wagons of all ages and shapes, which have been drawn up in corner, I
think I have secured it. I need shelter to day, for one quite loses
Ammergau and its people among masses of tourists, some of whom
are rude enough. The sun is kind! As I look resolutely at my picture, it falls full on the house, and makes most beautiful the vine
which, growing thick and green, forms an arbor over the seat just
outside the window, where Mayer is at work; it flashes through
the stiff fruit trees of the garden, and shows bits of the cottages
behind them. A young and lovely lady comes from the house, and
sits in my precious little arbor, book in hand. She is soon joined
by Mayer, and as they talk together—she evidently a lady of high
degree, he a rare but simple peasant—he bears the contrast well.
Yes! I can now make a drawing of the house as it is, with the broad
sunlight shining full on its inmate.

    In the afternoon I am by the theatre, which is thronged
with people choosing seats for the morrow. A motley crowd, sur-
rounds the building. There are sellers of all sorts of wares, holy
toys from the Tyrol, the Madonna and Child most numerous, wax
saints in glass cases, and photographs. There are pilgrims from
Jerusalem, selling beads of holy wood, and crosses of mother-of-
pearl, formed of twelve oblong tablets, and in the centre of each a
stone, to represent the twelve stations of Christ's sufferings. They
can speak only a few words in French, so they trade by writing
figures on a slate. Holy pictures and charms of every kind are to
be seen; and eatables there are, too, of various sorts, —cakes, cheese,
ham, bread and beer. As far as one can see along the Unter Ammergau road, come the peasant fruit-dealers from South Tyrol, with

* Sometimes spelled Maier. Joseph Mayer was well-known for portraying
Christ.

great baskets, or hand barrows, carried or drawn by women, who often have babies to care for besides, while the handsome husbands, enjoying a smoke, walk leisurely along, and now and then lend a helping hand! I must draw here on Saturday, that I may see something of the life outside the theatre. What a chance for a figure artist!

All around the little booths, under the great entrance, the peasants seem devoutly to believe in the efficacy of the charms they sell. One old fellow lauds rings of lead, with holy names inscribed thereon, as good for the cure of rheumatic joints. A lady asks the price of one of them. "Eighteen kreutzers, but they are worth eighteen guldens ten times over, gracious lady." "Now we know something, you and I," the lady answers, "and we know that the rings are not worth eighteen guldens." "You don't believe it, my dear lady? Ah! May God have mercy on you! Poor sufferers from all parts of the world send for them, and are made well! May you never have need of them!" I look in the lady's face, and find a dear friend, parted from long ago, amidst very different surroundings. She is staying at Sebastian Lang's, one of the best wood-carvers in the village, and after we have wandered a little longer, looking at the strange surrounding sights, I go with her to hear the violin played by her host and his young sons, whom he has himself taught. One might go far before having so great a treat as to see the splendid old man and his boys, and hear them play national airs and dances. The whole family seem wonderfully intelligent, and aware of what is going on in the outside world.

Now by the evening light, how delicious my work is! Just across the bridge, with my face towards the village, and my back to the Kofel, —at this hour in deepest shade, and sending down from its heights, like a faint spiritual voice from the evening sky, the sound of hymns sung by pilgrims, as they climb to worship at the foot of the cross, —I have the merry little river telling of its happiness to the clump of willows that fringe my bit of foreground, while its ripples play over the church and homestead reflected in its bosom.

Sunday morning, bright and clear. After a solemn service in the church, the children walk with the orchestra to the the-

atre. I do not dare to go there a second time, so I carry my books
up the mountain side, meeting on the way the cows coming home
for the morning milking time. There are at least a dozen of them
decked with garlands of bright flowers. My friend the herd tells
me that it is the name-day of their owner, and that for each cow
he receives a gift; and the creatures carry their heads proudly, as if
they knew it. It is a good climb before I find a seat, in a place
where the sweet summer air brings me the voices of the singers,
clear and soft from the valley down there, where the hearts of thousands of people worship. I can read but little. My memory is full
of the time when, in my own country, I first read of the
Passionsspiel, in Miss Howitt's Art Life in Munich.* I remember
well how shocked I felt, that any one could witness such a spec-
tacle; yet there was a fascination in her description of it, which
kept that chapter always in my mind! Eighteen years ago that must
be; and now I am living with, and loving, the people who were the
chief characters in the play of that very time.

　　　The smoke curling from many a chimney tells me that
dinner time is near, and that Francie will be at home, perhaps her
father also, and ready to talk to me awhile, before they go back
again for the long afternoon. The children come at twelve o'clock,
and say nothing to me of what they think. We eat together in si-
lence, but I see they are touched. When I meet them, after it is all
over, and we walk away into the quiet fields by the river side, I am
glad to hear them say that it was a reality almost too great for
them to bear, and never to be forgotten. The cattle are going out
again to pasture, ringing their sweet bells. All nature appears as
though wrapped in soothing peace. We talk of home, and of our
beloved ones there, and tears of longing for their presence cannot
be restrained.

---

* Anna Mary Howitt, *An Art-Student in Munich* (London, 1853).

IV.

OUR HOME WITH THE FLUNGERS.

Monday brings a new life to us. I have my work in my own room in the house of the Flungers. The fountain in front has much to do to-day. The Flunger family and three or four neighboring ones are incessant in their demands for fresh supplies; and it is a pleasure to see the response of the pure, ever-flowing water. The Flungers, —father, son, Francie, Sefie and Malie, the girl who helps so much in the fields, —have all gone to the hay meadows. It is very interesting to notice the people at their ordinary occupations, at their homes and in the fields, and think of them as they were seen only yesterday, standing before the large audiences in the Passion Theater. Yesterday, the admired of thousands; to-day, forgetting fame in their work in the hay-field or on the mountains. In the broad part of the valley, close by where the Wildbach flows, where the land is divided into many small patches, every householder of the village possesses one or more lots. Among the mowers are not only the men, but the women and maidens of the village; and Francie and Sefie swing their scythes with a grace and ease that show them to be adepts at the work.

  The labor of the girls when at home is also very exhausting, especially during this busy Passion year; for having to attend to so many guests, they do not get to bed until very late. In ordinary times, too, they are by no means idle, and when there is nothing to be done in the fields, they help Herr Flunger and Friedrich to carve little picture frames, Francie sawing out the forms from the rough wood, Friedrich, the father, or Malie carving them, leav-

ing Barbet to polish the carved frames. Malie is really a remarkable girl, plain and unassuming as she is. She can do and does the
finest parts of the wood-carving; her hand has the most craft, and
everything she touches goes well. She knows how to draw, and begins to take an interest in my work, as she finds that I am trying in
earnest to make my pictures like the real places. What a pity it is
that hard labor has long ago deprived her of the youthful fresh-
ness and gaiety that she once possessed; for when a child she was
much prettier than her sister Francie. But hard labor is woman's
lot in Ammergau, as well as in so many other parts of Germany,
though perhaps not to such a degree. On the Rhine you will meet
her toiling up the mountain side, groaning under a burden heavy
enough for a mule. In the neighborhood of the Taunus Mountains one meets gangs of half a hundred female day-laborers, who
have to work from sunrise to dark, for a paltry sum of little over
thirty kreuzers; and to keep them at work, a kind of slave-driver
has to superintend them. The women of Ammergau have, however, not so wretched a position as the latter; but they have to do
nearly all the out-door field-work; and they do it with a good will,
never thinking for a moment but that God intended it to be so.
The result is that feminine beauty is rarely found in the young
women of the village after they have reached twenty-five; and later
in life they become coarse in form and feature, in feeling and manner, and their original loveliness disappears.*

Life is most interesting among these people, if one can
adopt their way of living; but to fret because one has not home
comforts would make a hard condition of life. The children have
gone to the hay-field, with a pleasant English party, people who,

---

* The women of Oberammergau have become more assertive. Tradition
forbade women older than thirty-five from appearing on stage, but law-
suits have now forced the abandonment of this restriction. The role of
the Virgin Mary was regularly played by an unmarried woman of un-
blemished character, which sometimes led to the anomalous situation
where the woman playing Mary was younger than her son. In 1990, for
the first time, a married woman with her own children, Elisabeth Petre,
played the role of the Virgin Mary.

THE CHURCHYARD GATE

like us, have adapted themselves to the ways of the family, and
beautify everything by their unselfish forbearance. I draw in the
afternoon by the house of Caiaphas, one of the Langs. It is the
most brilliantly frescoed edifice in the village. "Caiaphas" passes
in and out with stately step; his face is full of intelligence, and
wears a happy, contented expression. His children are very sweet;
the eldest girl, a quiet little maiden of nine or ten summers, watches
over the two younger ones, and knits her stocking on the bench
beside me. Herr Lang takes the part of Caiaphas with great abil-
ity, and having enjoyed a better education than most of the people
of Ammergau, he is a prominent personage in the village. In the
dramatical affairs his voice has great influence.

There is a fountain at a little distance from us, and a great
gathering of women about it. I hear loud talking, while tubs and
dishes are washed. Money is the great theme; and I hear quite
enough to be sure that there is a gossipy sort of conversation going on. I look around for a quieter place; but this is the spot, and
here I must bide; for there are three capital bits, front, right and
left of me, and the afternoon sun gives wonderful effects of light
and shade. By this time I begin to find out that there is gossip in
the village, and I must not try to escape the knowledge of it: so I
will call the sketch in front of the house of Caiaphas—"The Gossips' Fountain."

In vain! It is impossible to do anything with the house
of "Petrus"! There is not a bit of vine, nor a tree, to break its
utter monotony. I talk with its owner, Jacob Hett, and he tells me
that he will help me in any way he can; but there is the house, and
what can one do? So I go off, and idle with the young people at
home; but as it begins to rain, and grows miserably cold, we all go
into the living-room, where we find the family, and some Dutch
artists, who have just arrived. Our grand room is by this time oc-
cupied by two elderly ladies, who keep entirely apart, and never
see nor speak to the family, unless they want something. But we
have cheerful company, and Hans plays the zither. We talk with
the Dutch artists, of the great pictures at the Hague, of the wood-
carving of the village, of the monks of Ettal, who did so much

for Art, especially in this direction, of former years of the Passion Play, and the various characters who had performed in it. I think of the party up stairs, and how much they miss by bringing their city conventionalities with them so far into the mountains.

We had a time of real pleasure, and in the evening came the English lesson, which lasted till eleven. Francie was Nora's pupil, Sefie Nellie's. The letters came first—a, b, c—no sooner learnt than forgotten again. Then came the effort to name objects, cat, dog, cow, and this was more successful. Sefie was clever at whole sentences, "How do you do?" "Have you slept well?" Then there was great fun when the pupils were put to conversation together. Francie to Sefie—"You hev plue eis ant brown hair"—Sefie to Francie: "Goot morning, have you slept well?" "Pretty well tank you." Teacher: "Now try to say the *th*." At this point I cover my ears, for when teachers and pupils get to work at this one sound, it is too much! These lessons are given three days in each week, and every night when the young girls go down stairs, I hear them go over all they have learnt to their mother. Next day I find that great progress has been made by the girls in their lingual studies, for I am greeted with, "Good e-ven-ing, are you very tight (tired) to-night?" The great stumbling-block of the *th* is a little removed.

Friday Morning. — Still cloudy! So after we have been to the early service in the church, the girls go out to search for a model, but as all the grown and strong people are hard at work in the hay-fields, they are obliged to be content with anything they can find. I go to the post-office to ask for letters, and as I enter the yard, I see the back of Peter's house, picturesque as it is odd, with the carriage way leading up to the barn of the post-house. It is a happy discovery, and I lose no time in getting to work, as I must have the house of the good Peter. Jacob Hett himself carries out my chair for me, and I sit in state under the great poplar tree, in front of which, but outside the railing, the fruit dealers are building their stalls, and arranging tempting fruits for to-morrow's throng of customers. The dialect they employ is harsh; and I cannot imagine a single word of love spoken in it. Certainly, what I hear around

me now must be anything but kindly! When I return home, I find a studio arranged near the door of the barn, and two old women of the village being made into pictures by very diligent students. After dinner we all go together to my new study—the house of the Scribe. The owner is quite in keeping with his dwelling, which is saying a good deal—for the house is in truth an original study.

Saturday Evening. — As we come home through the village, the outer world is rushing in to our quiet nest. A lovely evening loses all its poetry in the noise of the travellers, who, hungry and thirsty, and in need of rest, pass up and down the crowded streets, looking for their places. I chat with the women outside, who stand with babies in their arms, watching the new arrivals. Maier's house progresses; to-day I make the acquaintance of his wife and children. The latter have a little maid called Pinosa to wait upon them, as the mother has much to do. A crowd passes in and out of the house all the morning. Some push in merely from curiosity, others to get autographs, or to ask questions, some few to do a kindness to Maier by ordering carved work. One lady brings a piece of white drapery for the tableau of the Resurrection in the play, another an old engraving, which the man's Art education enables him to value. The door stands wide open all day long, and the wife tells me that her husband is often kept up till midnight on Saturdays, which is but a poor preparation for the next day's exhaustion, —a day, too, on which he fasts from all solid food.

Sunday. — It is too crowded to do anything outside the theatre to-day, so I spend my whole afternoon down by the river, towards Unter Ammergau, and find it really fascinating there. On this occasion we have a party, some of our visitors being dear friends whom we found among the throng of new comers. The talk with them about our home has a strange effect, so utterly is that home in the distance, in spirit as well as in space. The description of the difficulties they have had to-day in getting food at the Post Inn is really comic. One of the ladies went into the kitchen, seized plates from a dark corner, washed them at the pump in the yard, then,

armed with a fork, made her way to the cooking stove, and succeeded in carrying off sausages and potatoes enough for the whole party. Brown bread, cheese, and beer, were the possibilities, but meat and vegetables were only to be had by people of great resolution. Every fresh bend of the river gives a new picture, and the one on which I decide is to be the Going Away from Ober-Ammergau. The theater lies low, at the foot of the distant mountains, while the river winds around and under the mighty Kofel with a graceful sweep. But before I make this drawing, there is one I take great pleasure in thinking of. It is the Churchyard Gate, which stands always open, and through which every morning after early mass I see the aged Geistlicher Rath Daisenberger pass. I begin to hear his name mentioned with great love and respect by the people.

Another lovely Sabbath day has come and gone. The morning which we spent in the garden was still and calm. Not a soul to be seen in the street, except the old men, who, wearing blue and white badges on their arms, walked up and down the village during the "Spiel." They are too old to take any part in the representation, so they watch over the quiet of the place, marching two together, with a very important air, which says, "We also do something." The play is over at six o'clock; when we go for our evening walk, and look down from the lovely hill-side, at the back of the Flunger house, in pity for the restless crowd pouring out of our home. Many come to our garden to have supper, and it is always late before we go in for ours on Sunday evenings. There is no one this week to join our party, except our artist friends, who think of the day's sight as we do; and so it forms a bond of union between us. I remark how full of respect their manner is to the young women of the house. It is great pain to me to hear all the flatteries adressed to Francie and Sefie, and to know that they must have their effect, particularly at a time when life is so unsettled with them.

VIEW FROM THE HOUSE OF "CAIAPHAS"

V.

AN APOSTOLIC FAMILY.

At work in the street in front of the school-house! My subject is the house of the Zwinks, the owner of which, Matthew Zwink, takes the part of St. Matthew in the Passion Play, and his son Johannes, that of the youthful St. John. The group of young pupils around me are more enthusiastic about the portraits they are taking in doors, of father and son, than about the old house that covers them. But I find that the latter has also strong characteristics, —a roof rugged with age; walls seamed and cracked all over, and bending in and out in quite a reckless way; the gutters of the roof stretching out to an enormous length beyond the eaves; and a dilapidated fence, of most independent build, pretending to take care of the pretty things in the garden. In the distance is the very oldest house in Ammergau. Its interior, especially the kitchen, is very extraordinary, and contains a deep well, an arched roof, and a chimney with a long shaft, running up to the sky. I am told that this house is at least six hundred years old, and has been standing ever since the time when Ammergau was one of the stations on the great highway of travel for the merchandise from Venice to Augsburg and the north of Germany, and when all the caravans passing through the valley had to make halt at Ammergau for the night and over Sunday. I am told that even in the days of the Romans,*

---

* Excavations have in fact unearthed artifacts from Roman times, indicating the importance of the trade route through the village. The "isolation" of this Alpine village is therefore something of a myth. Now, because of the play and its many visitors, it is sometimes known as "the most sophisticated village in Germany."

Ammergau was a known station on their military road, from
Partenkirchen northwards, and was then known as Coveliacas, a
name doubtless derived from the guardian peak of the village, —
our good Kofel. But I am forgetting the Zwinks. As soon as we
were visible, the entire family, consisting of the mother, father, aunt,
and the son Johannes, came out to bid us welcome. The son is a
generous-minded youth, of refined and gentle nature, well fitting
him to take the part of St. John in the play. It is pleasant to see
the affection of the mother and aunt for their boy. The good Matthew tells me, in reply to my inquiries, all about the remarkable
frescoes on the houses of the village, many of which were painted
by his grandfather, between the years 1780 and 1790. He says that
the artist was not always allowed to choose his own subject, this being done by the owner of the house himself, and the results are very
odd. Zwink also painted some of the frescoes in the village church, as
well as in the church at Ettal.* After the older Zwink had told me all
this, I turned to listen to Johannes, who spoke of being obliged to
fulfil his military duties. He thinks, naturally enough, that the barracks will be a poor exchange for the mountain climbs and the pure
air of his Highland home. It is, indeed, pleasant to find such kindness everywhere. The family have now brought out chairs and foot-
stools, so that we can work more comfortably. I rejoice over our
present felicity, as I contrast it with the martyrdom which we
suffered at the hands of rude butcher-boys and ignorant market-
women last summer in the streets of Nuremberg. We are invited
to return in the evening, when there will be music in the house.

Extract from Nellie's Note Book. — This is the King's birthday,
and a general holiday.† There was high mass in the church this

---

* See the splendidly illustrated book *Franz Seraph Zwink: Der Luftmaler von
Oberammergau* (Oberammergau, 1986). Though Greatorex is well aware of
these open-air frescoes on the village homes, they are barely perceptible
in her sketches.

† Ludwig II, King of Bavaria, was born in 1845 and reigned from 1864 to
1886. Much has been written about the allegedly "mad" Ludwig. A recent

morning, and I went with Sefie and Francie into the choir. Francie had to take the part of the principal soprano, in place of Julie Albl, who, we heard, had suddenly lost her father, the head and principal support of a large family. Poor Julie! Notwithstanding her great grief, she must occupy her usual place in the Chorus on Sunday, since it cannot be filled by any other girl of the village. She has a most beautiful soprano voice, and charms the Passion audiences by the purity and reach of her song. She is rather a peculiar girl. She became tired of the world a few years ago, and, principally because she possessed such a beautiful voice, she was accepted in a cloister, in the neighborhood of Augsburg. But when the committee were selecting persons to take the various parts in the Passion Play of 1870, they found great difficulty in selecting a first soprano for the Chorus, the only person available being Francie Flunger, who was needed more urgently, however, to delineate the character of the Virgin. Since strangers are not permitted to take any part in the Passion Play, the committee decided upon inducing Julie to return to the village. It was not without considerable difficulty and expense, however, that the community succeeded in inducing the superioress of the convent to give up the nightingale she had secured.

At night we all went to the house of the Zwinks, to hear the promised concert. We were ushered into a large, low room, in one corner of which stood the great, green porcelain stove, with a broad bench all round it, where the people sit in the long winter evenings. About a small table, on which lay some music, the musicians, four violins and a bass, had already taken their places. Johannes and his parents came to greet us, and gave us comfortable seats. We were not the only guests. Two women, relations of the family, sat on the bench by the stove. They were naturally large

account is *The Mad King: A Biography of Ludwig II of Bavaria* (Secaucus, N.J., 1996) by Greg King. Clearly a romantic eccentric, if not actually insane, Ludwig was fascinated by the Oberammergau Passion Play. He had a command performance for himself, described in chapters 7 and 8 below, because he did not like to appear in public.

THE HOME OF THE VILLAGE

women, but the plaited skirts, padded waists, and wide sleeves of
their splendid peasant costume, made them appear to be of immense size. They were evidently tired from the long journey they
had made to the Passion Play, and so we could excuse the little
naps they took by stealth, while the music was going on. The concert was very effective, most of the pieces played being from the
masses of Dedler,* who composed and added to the music of the
Passion. Before leaving our hosts we had arranged a party to go
up the Kofel, and to the Bürschling mountain, where the King of
Bavaria has a hunting lodge, called the Linderhof.

I must state something that happened the other day. We
had gone to the Zwink house, to join Johannes and two ladies in
an excursion to Altenau, which we had decided must be the
Almenau of "Quits." But the ladies had the bad news for us, that
it could not be the same place, since there is no churchyard there.
So we gave up the projected journey, and to make up for our disappointment, Johannes promised to sit for us, while we drew his
portrait. So we darkened all the numerous windows but one, and
were engaged intently upon our work, when we were startled by
hearing a woman's voice, calling out, "Where is St. John? Where
is St. John?" The door opened, and a short, portly old dame, whose
tiny black eyes sparkled from behind her glasses, followed by two
pretty young girls, rushed into the room. Frau Zwink said, very
quietly, pointing to our subject, "This is my son Johannes!" The
little old lady stopped short before the object of her search, and
she and her daughters had a good stare at him, for fully two minutes. They were so interested in him, that they never thought of
addressing a word to the poor fellow, who had risen from his seat,
and stood like a statue under their gaze. "He's very like his photograph," at last the old lady exclaimed, and turning round, she left

---

* Rochus Dedler, 1779–1822, was the village schoolmaster. He composed
a number of orchestral pieces and much religious music in addition to
the passion play music. See Clemens Haertle-Dedler, *Rochus Dedler: Der
Komponist der Passionsmusik zu Oberammergau* (Oberammergau, 1979).

the room, followed by her daughters, as unceremoniously as she had entered it, shutting the door with a bang. Johannes stood for a minute like one dazed, and then, when he saw us laughing joined in with good will. This is the way tourists frequently "do up" the principal players of Ammergau.

The Linderhof. — We have just returned from our excursion to the King's hunting lodge at the top of the Bürschling mountain. We left the village in the early morning, each carrying sketch-book, alpine stock, and provisions for the day. We joined the two ladies and Johannes, and reached the foot of the Kofel just as the mountains became flushed with the dawn. We had a difficult climb, till near the top, then an easy ascent till we reached Bürschling, finishing with a hard pull, that lasted till mid-day, when we arrived at the Royal Hunting Lodge. On the way we saw only one solitary woman, who was carrying provisions up to the Senner,* who lived yet higher up on the mountain, and in whose hut, she told us, we could have milk, and rest ourselves. But we were already tired, so we seated ourselves, and enjoyed our lunch, and the lovely view among the mountains, and along the valley, winding in and out, longing only to reach the snow that seemed so near us, —for it was very hot, and we found but little shelter. It was so very lonely, that I wondered that any one could stay there; but I am told that the King is very fond of such quiet romantic spots, where he goes to escape the cares of government, that must weigh sometimes rather heavily upon his shoulders, and to spend his solitary hours in reading or in study. We sketched the scenery, and Johannes made quite a pretty picture of the royal lodge itself, which mother says is pretty enough to find a place in her collections.

Our visit to the Senner was brief, but Nora, who is fond of such novelties, describes him "as a perfect beauty for a sketch, —an old man, his name Tony, with shaggy grey hair, coming down

----

* A Senner is a mountain herdsman who makes extra money selling dairy products directly to hikers.

OUTSIDE THE PASSION THEATER

into his eyes, and mixing with his eyebrows, which are an inch long; a beard, whiskers, and moustache hiding all his face except two little bits of what looked like dark red leather drawn tightly over the cheek-bones; his coat of some knitted stuff, a splendid dirty blue, torn and patched to a high degree; a well-worn and very dirty, peaked hat, of dark green, with coarse worsted cord and tassel hanging over the rim, right in front of the forehead: the picture being quite complete when he took the churn-dash in his hand."

The return home was very easy and agreeable. We were a happy party, and enjoyed ourselves freely. When we arrived in the charming valley of Grasswang, we washed away the stains of travel at the bubbling springs which we found there. The entire valley is one of the loveliest of the Highlands. Johannes told us that the last King of Bavaria, Max,* inspired by beauty of the scenery, expressed the wish that the Ammergau Passion theatre should be erected at the entrance of the valley. We had quite a talk as we came along the valley, and Johannes told us how it was that he came to be chosen to represent St. John in the Passion Play; how that three others had been considered as elegible for the position, but that he was finally selected. One of his rivals was allotted the part of the servant of Pilatus, the other, that of the servant of King Herod who puts the white mantle on "Christus." The selection of persons for the various roles is done by the vote of all the householders of the village sitting in committee, under the presidency of the Geistlicher Rath Daisenberger, and the priest. It is very rarely that a bad selection is made. Johannes told us that he had never received any dramatic instruction, except from the Geistlicher Rath, and yet he acts the part of St. John very naturally, and without any effort. He told us that his father (the present St. Matthew) had taken the part of St. John in the year 1840, that of Peter in 1850, of James the elder in 1860, and in 1870 and 1871

---

* Maximilian II of Bavaria, 1811–64, reigned from 1848 to 1864 and was the father of Ludwig II.

that of Matthew; and that his grand-father had taken the part of the Christus in the years 1800, 1801, 1810 and 1815, and of Peter in 1820, 1830 and 1840. The talent for the apostolic rôles seems therefore to be hereditary in the family. Many people think that Johannes will have to be the "Christus" of the next Passion Play, in 1880.*

* Selection of the director and the players has sometimes had a distinctly political character. Factions in the village sometimes contend with each other, while well-established families seek to maintain control of roles that have traditionally been in the family. The election of the director for the 2000 play was a hotly contested race in 1998, won by Christian Stückl, director, and a group of reformers, including Otto Huber.

THE GOSSIP'S FOUNTAIN

VI.

THE HOUSE OF GREGOR LECHNER.

From beside a cottage, in whose shadow there lies a pile of logs on a bit of green roadside, I look up the street where Gregor Lechner, the "Judas," has his house, the pale green tint of which makes a severe contrast to the dark reddish-brown one beside it, which has apparently enjoyed for ages immunity from "cleaning up." The usual mound, of right belonging to the barn-yard, is near the door, but on the top of it grow some brilliant weeds; and there is a graceful tree whose shadow falls on the sunny porch. It was not easy to find a seat among the logs, so I went into the house, to make myself known to Frau Lechner, and to beg for a chair; and I got not only the very best one she had, but also one of the great "nudels" which she was cooking for the frugal dinner, with the wish that I might eat it "with a good appetite," which I did. I sat by the work-bench of Gregor Lechner himself, who was very busily engaged in finishing some carved statuettes, especially one of himself, in the character of "Judas." His principal work is the carving of the "Descent from the Cross," after Rubens'* celebrated picture. He is also famed for his carvings of figures for the "Weihnachtskrippen,"† being one of the most skillful workmen in the village, as he is perhaps the best actor, dramatically speaking, and one of the best informed on general and dramatic subjects.

---

* Peter Paul Rubens, 1577–1640, was a Flemish painter.

† Christmas crèche scenes.

I had hardly finished my "nudel" before Herr Flunger and
the Dutch artists came in. The latter are delighted with the village, and will sketch here for a week yet. It was very interesting to
hear Flunger and Lechner talk together. A warm affection seems
to exist between these two men, and while they talked about the
Passionsspiel, the tears came into Lechner's eyes, as he told how
that on the previous Monday, one of the visitors had said in the
photograph store, that he wanted the portraits of all the principal
players except "Judas," who, he said, must be a very bad man, or
he could not play the part so perfectly.*

Poor man! He has indeed much to suffer from the rude
criticisms of the ignorant, especially of the peasants of the neighboring Tyrol, who look upon Judas in the true Middle Age spirit
as the incarnation of all that is wicked! Lechner says that he was
once stopped on the road between Unter-Ammergau and his home,
by a party of half-drunken Tyrolese, who used hard words to him,
and he thinks would have killed him had he not made good his
escape. In former years, these rough peasants would express themselves very freely about the players, even while the drama was being given; and one, who had become excited and indignant that
Judas should betray his Master, stood up in the midst of the audience, and shook his fists at the betrayer, and shouted out, "If I
could but get hold of thee, thou rascal, I would teach thee some-

---

* The version of the passion play that Greatorex saw was presented with
few major changes until 1960. The idea that "the Jews" in general, and
Judas in particular, were the villains of the piece, reflects an old Christian
myth. Jews had been accused of "deicide," the murder of God, since the
Middle Ages, and that accusation was used to justify anti-Jewish prejudices even during the Holocaust. Since the Vatican II Council of the
1960s, the Roman Catholic Church has maintained that it is unjust to
blame "the Jews" for the suffering and death of Christ. In important
reforms for the 1990 play, carried even further in 2000, the leaders of the
Oberammergau community have moved away from the earlier, anti-Jewish interpretation. See Gordon R. Mork, "'Wicked Jews' and 'Suffering
Christians' in the Oberammergau Passion Play," in *Representations of Jews
through the Ages* (Creighton University Press, 1996), 153–69.

thing!" Lechner has given the character of Judas in the Passion
Play ever since the year 1850, with three different persons representing the "Christus." Though he does not say so, he seems to
remember with most pleasure the time when Tobias Flunger was
the principal character; while he admits that Joseph Maier has
the best presence and voice. Schauer, who was the "Christus"
of the play of 1860, was a very beautiful personification, but he
had not strength of mind to resist all the flattery he received from
visitors.

I learnt all this from Lechner, after the others had gone;
as also, that his father had played the part of Judas in the years
1830 and 1840. When I asked him, if he had not received special
instruction from his father, how to give the character to such per-
fection, he said, No, he had not received instruction from any one
then, but had, as long as he could remember, lived in the thought
of how to do it, and imagining, while watching his father act, the
changes he would make in the representation. He said, further,
that after the Geistlicher Rath Daisenberger came to the village,
and wrote the part for Judas anew, in blank verse, he had private
rehearsals in the good priest's house for some time, as had all the
principal players, —and that was in reality their only dramatic
school. Envious people, he said, had sent abroad the report that
he and others had studied dramatic gesticulation in Munich, during the winter preceding the play of 1870, but the assertion was
entirely false. Lechner called to mind the fact, that when the celebrated dramatist Eduard Devrient* came to the Passion Play in
1850, he had praised the acting as not excelled by any regular actors, and had said, "We (actors) can learn much from them."

Lechner has many pleasant memories of the visits to his
little cottage of prominent dramatic personages, who seek up the
"Judas" as soon as they arrive in the village, since his fame is now
very great. And yet with all this flattery he is not at all vain. When I

---

* Devrient was a German actor, impresario, and theater historian. He
helped make the play famous with a report on the 1850 performance, *Das
Passion Schauspiel im Dorfe Oberammergau in Oberbayern* (Leipzig, 1851).

THE GATHERING OF THE BAND

translated him a sentence which I found in one of the large English papers, that "the acting of Gregor Lechner would be considered brilliant on any court stage of Europe," he said he was very glad indeed to find that foreigners appreciated him, for he thought that the villagers did not. He loves to talk of the drama, and thinks with great pleasure, too, of the secular plays that have been performed by the Ammergauers in previous summers, especially of a Christmas play about six years ago, when persons came to the village on Christmas Eve from a distance of over twenty miles to see it. Noticing Lechner's bright little boy, who is one of the genii in the second tableau of the play, the "Adoration of the Cross," I asked the father if he intended that Anton should take his father's present part, when he grew up. "No! No!" he said, "I will spare Anton the annoyance that I have had to suffer on account of Judas Iscariot!" Little Anton, too, shook his head, and said "Nein!" One must admire Lechner much for the self-abnegation that he must condescend to during the play: for while most of the other principal players have to represent characters higher than their own original natures, he has to personify a character which he at heart despises. Lechner is one of the most pious men of the village. He is now tolerably comfortable in his means, owning the house in which he lives, a few plots of meadow land, and two cows, all of which—house, meadow and cows, —are attended to by Frau Lechner; while he sits industriously at his work-table, in ordinary times from half past four in the morning till dusk, or from fifteen to sixteen hours a day, and all for a sum not exceeding a Prussian thaler!

I left him after this conversation with a feeling of respect and admiration; and will do the best I can to make the pea-green house a picture for his sake. When I carried home my borrowed chair, the door of the room was open into the large hall, and I saw Gregor Lechner asleep at his work-bench. His wife was in the kitchen, so I passed on there, and she told me that her husband was very tired. He has such a hard part, and on Sundays, when the story is told, he comes home sometimes quite exhausted. Then she

told me, but not complainingly, that these two summers of the Passion Play have been also hard on her. She has had no help but that of her little boy. To be sure many good people waited on them-selves, but others would have even warm baths carried up her little crooked staircase, until her back was weary and her feet would go no more. She laughed while telling me that once the great tub fell from her hands just as she was half way down, and another time the gentleman upset his own India-rubber bath, and the water ran down into her kitchen over everything, and then he took her fine plumeau to stand on. I asked permission for the children to make a drawing of her little kitchen, which is a picture of neatness, and she thought this a great honor. Her "man" and her "boy" are all to her in life, the good woman says, and she likes to keep the house bright for them.

Wash-day in the Village. — There is a great time among the women ever Tuesday morning, when they bring their washing down to the river's bank. The favorite place is just opposite the priest's house, in the heart of the village, and the prettiest bit of it all, where the Ammer runs clear and cold as ice on the hottest summer day; and there the artists congregate for the two last days of the week. Flunger tells me that he once counted fifteen of them drawing at the same time. The door-way of the priest's house is the chosen spot, and as I take my seat there, he, coming up, exclaims, "Dear lady, are you also drawing our Kofel? If this goes on much longer, there will be nothing of it left. Every one who comes here must needs try to take it." So, laughingly, I say, I will take pity on the mountain, and on his fears, and crossing the road towards the pretty garden, I find for myself a picture with more of the water, and the village. The washer-women, among them two sisters of the good priest, are so gay as they dip, and splash, and rub, and wring their white linen and red and white checked plumeau covers, that I long to sketch them, and to make my picture a bright one, but my pen will not obey my wish. The children return from school, and, bring-ing their toys into the garden where I sit, play about me. I love to

have them come to see what I am doing, and put their plump little hands into mine, unasked, with the utmost simplicity, and the sweetest air imaginable.

We have a merry party at supper. The artist trio bring in their sketches in pencil and water-color, and there is a great comparing of studies, and "wonderment" at the odd things each has found for himself. The lamps are brought out to the long table in the garden where we sit. Flunger is with us, and we have a very interesting conversation, in which he joins. I venture to ask how, after so many years of life among the Munich artists, he can bear the life he now leads? He simply answers, "For me life has always had a heavy shadow side, and I like better the country than the city shadow. If I can live in my quiet home, at my peaceful work, I am content."

To-day I take leave, with much pleasure, of my corner opposite the Gossips' Fountain. It is the one evil spot in the whole village, and the people tell me that the house near it is truly the only one in which discord reigns. The one woman who lives there goes in and out the live-long day, with matted hair and disorderly dress, scolding in shrill voice, and with violent gestures, her unhappy men, who retort angrily. Yet she can be very entertaining, I feel sure, as I watch her chattering to the women who come to clean and fill their vessels at the fountain. Heads come close together in earnest talk, and then there is a lingering, and a turning back again to say another word before they part, with that sinking of the voice and shaking of the head as they get deep into the conversation, which there is no mistaking, and which assures me that I have not given my drawing a wrong title!

I have just made the acquaintance of Frau Veit, who has filled an important position here this summer, from the great trouble she has taken in procuring accommodation for strangers, to many of whom her kindness has been invaluable at such a time, and in many cases especially so from her being able to speak French fluently. Her husband follows the usual calling of the villagers, wood-carving, and they have one of the best shops for it in their house, which is very old and still retains the name of "The Kastner

House," from having been, during the prosperous times of the Ettal monastery, the depository of its "bread and flour chest"* at Ober-Ammergau. I have decided that this edifice too shall be included among my Homes!

* The *Kasten* is literally the casket or box in which the valuables are held, and the *Kastner* is the householder who watches over it.

VII.

THE CLOSE OF THE PASSION PLAY.

It is now drawing towards the end of the Passion season; and while my life and work grow more and more absorbing, it seems more difficult to write about them. The crowds increase, the work in the houses is harder, the women have great toil, and the men are obliged to give up all attempts at wood-carving, while they gather in the scanty harvest. In our home I find the same kindness to strangers, and the same affection for us. I admire the character of Flunger more than ever, and greatly enjoy my frequent meetings with Maier. We invited Frau Maier and her little girl a few days since to make an excursion with us to Partenkirchen and Garmisch. The day proved charming, and the beautiful valley of Grasswang, along which we went was too lovely for any word-painting of mine. The mountains, reaching up into the far heavens, wore their glorious robes of blue and snow-white, while their trains of velvet mossy green were lost in graceful foldings, among the beautiful trees of the valley. It was a new sensation for us to find ourselves once more in places of fashionable resort, such as Partenkirchen and Garmisch. After a good lunch, and a sight of many finely dressed ladies, we turned our faces homewards, satisfied that our own village was the best place in summer, and that if the scenery was not so fine as that around Partenkirchen, the people more than compensate for the difference.

It is charming to see in this village the almost universal abandonment of aristocratic conventionalities. I shall never forget one family—an English clergyman, his lady, sister, and niece, — who resided for ten days in our house. Refined and delicate in all

THE HOUSE OF JOSEPH MAIER ("CHRISTUS")

their tastes, they did not stand aside as mere spectators of the family life, but shared it as far as was possible. They brought their pretty sewing into our living room in the evenings, listened with pleasure to the zither-playing of Hans and the singing of the Flunger maidens; and in return, sang for us sweet chorals and English ballads. The children said that the haying parties lost their charm when they went away, and the women missed the tall, handsome gentleman who would always help them with their heavy loads through the garden. —Among the Schutzgeister* of the Passion Play, the sweetest face and the most winning manners belong to Josepha Flunger, our Sefie. Many have been the compliments addressed her, during the summer; yet she has remained simple and unspoiled until now. This week has, however, been an eventful one in her life. Her betrothal has been announced in the house and throughout the village, as is the custom in Germany. Yet, I think Flunger himself is uneasy about the suddenness of the affair, and gives his consent reluctantly; but he has been overpowered by all the women, his wife in particular, who is quite taken with the good looks and manners of the young bridegroom, and with his intention of settling down in the village close by them. The girl is so truly good and modest, that I trust sincerely he may prove himself worthy of her. We are all invited to attend the wedding, at Christmas, and the children are to be bridesmaids.

After dinner Flunger came to take his coffee by the table where I sat writing, and seemed much depressed. I wanted him to take some commissions for carved work, to be done for me by Christmas; but he said that this was impossible. He told me that the last two summers have certainly brought to himself and to his family great pleasure, but also great labor and fatigue. The work in the fields, in all weather, hot or wet, was very trying to them, when, at the end of each week, they had to return to an unquiet house, irregular meals, and beds in the hay-loft.† The Passions-

---

* Guardian angels.

† Many residents gave up their own bedrooms to paying guests and slept in attics or haylofts during the play season.

spiel* is in itself most exhausting; and he spoke sadly of the exposure of his family to all kinds of exaggerated praise, and to temp-
tations to vanity from people of the world, as well as of the entire
breaking up of home life. He looked forward to all the labor that
is to be done around the house and in the fields and woods, and
added, It will be long after the snow comes before we can get to
wood-carving again. As I looked at the man, I thought, How full
of dignity and repose his manner, how full of character his face,
and that in his working dress he looks a noble man. He seemed
pleased when I told him how happy I have been in the village, and
how much I like his family, the two younger girls and Malie especially, and that it would give me great pleasure to see them all in
winter at Munich.

The mild days of September are drawing to a close, and
we are beginning to think of saying farewell to the Ammer vale,
and of gathering up souvenirs of our summer's sojourn here. We
had so often delighted in rambles over the rocks, especially those
at the foot of the Kofel, and we thought that if we could only
bring away a bit of the very growth of the hill itself, it would re-
mind us often, through the dark winter time in the city, of our
walks and climbs and long rests on the soft springy moss. So, en-
listing a little guide in our service, we took a broad basket and an
old knife, and followed the road winding round to Grasswang.
There is a sort of valley hollowed out, just where the ascent to the
Kofel begins, and where the goats belonging to the village are
guarded by their small herd-boy. Here we found the finest bunches
of ferns and fairy moss-cups, with many a trailing vine worthy of
becoming designs for the daintiest embroidery. We suffered as those
to whom fate is too lavish of her treasures generally do; for no
sooner had we filled our basket with one kind of moss, than another variety, lovelier and richer, caught our eyes, and tempted our
grasping hands; but at last we turned homewards. A little stream
ran by the road, and here, deep down in its mossy nooks, hiding
from the light frosts that catch and wilt their unsheltered sisters,

* Passion play.

THE CHURCH: BEYOND THE AMMER

grew the loveliest forget-me-nots. We must have a posy, and our little guide, ready to answer our asking looks, ventures down close to the water, too close! for with a splash and a tumble, she is in the stream. But what would be a severe fright to a city child, is only a joke to our little mountain maid, and with a clever spring and a merry laugh, she is again on dry ground, her hands filled with the precious wild-flowers. We get home, and begin to arrange our treasures, Francie and Malie telling us they know where much finer mosses are to be had, and that as soon as the field-work is done, they will send us some.

Sunday, September 24. — This morning was most beautiful, and the village all peaceful when I passed through it on my way to the fields, full now of the pale purple "prophet of the harvest" or autumn crocus, and where many of the cattle from the mountains now graze. It was the first Sunday that I had passed this way, and a most extraordinary sight it was, to see the groups of players in costume come out to rest on the seats behind the theatre. A sudden rain-storm drove me homewards. I found the church doors open, and a few women, who had been preparing dinner for their guests, came in to rest and pray for a little while. This little church has a feeling of home to me now, as it has been long a place of prayer, when passing on my way to my daily work. I listen to the music of the Passionsspiel, —the last that will be heard for ten long years to come.

Monday. — Yet once more the well known music awoke us this morning. The King had telegraphed to know if the play could not be repeated; and the answer was, "Yes, and we will give the proceeds to the wounded!" All summer I had resisted the strong desire to see the play a second time, fearing that familiarity with the people might destroy my first impression; yet it was with great regret that I saw the crowd disperse yesterday, after what we all thought was the last representation; so, to-day, I decided on venturing to look at it again. And now I thank the young King heartily for the opportunity of so doing, as, far from detracting from

my first impressions, it has been to me a real and pure enjoyment. All alone, from the furthest corner of the theatre, I watched for the parts I loved the best, the tableau of the Manna in the Wilderness, the scenes of the Last Supper, and the Betrayal. And while I recognised each individual of the great crowd, not one sweet or rugged face brought with it an unpleasant remembrance; but rather, with all the wonderful beauty of their pictures mingled that of the kindly greetings and gentle deeds of the long summer I had spent among them. —I am struck with the absence of all ostentation in the character of the principal men here. I have never heard them boast of their success. They seem to lose all personal feeling, in that of the honor paid to their drama. They are all delighted that the King should have honored their play with his presence; knowing that the young monarch has a high appreciation of the drama.

I have just been to Maier's house, to take coffee with Nora, and Maier and his wife entertained us for over an hour. They showed us the ring which the Prince of Wales* gave to Maier; they seem to value it very much, "for the sake of little Johanna," as the mother says, "who will be proud of it!" Maier is a man who has evidently thought much, and speaks with great freedom on many subjects. His affection and veneration for his spiritual father and teacher, the Geistlicher Rath, are very great. His own father died when he was very young, and he has always had to work hard. I asked him if he liked his work? He said Yes, and most of all the carving of flowers. His wife and children are his joy; and he never wishes to leave the village in which he was born. Only yesterday, he refused the offer of a large sum of money to go to England next summer. It makes one shiver to think of such wicked speculation. "Only think of it," said his wife, "that would make us rich; but Joseph would not do it for all the gold and silver in the mountains!" I believe that his life is a continual prayer to be made worthy of his position. I was much touched by a remark of Walter's, when we spoke of a former "Christus," who must have been a much more

---

* The future Edward VII of Great Britain attended the play in 1871.

THE HOUSE OF GREGOR LECHNER ("JUDAS")

beautiful personation of the character. "Ah!" said the boy, "but he had not the sorrow in his face that Maier has." And the remark has much truth in it. Later in the evening, Nora and I went down to the living room, when Maier and his wife sang for us some melodies of the Tyrol. Afterwards, Maier himself sang a famous Dutch song, with a splendid voice. We talked of the winter, and heard about the gay times of the wood-cutting in the forest and the dragging it home down the mountains; then of the wood-carving, and how it became the chief occupation of the villagers. Many orders have been left in the village for work to be done this winter, and I have been surprised, on looking over the designs in the different work shops, to see how much talent the carvers show.

September 29. — The church bells woke us early, and we heard chanting in the street. A procession soon appeared; first the boys of the village, with banners; then the old and young men; and after them the old and young women! Their voices, as they recited their prayers, were full and musical. They were going to Ettal, to give thanks for the harvest. To-morrow, another procession will come from Unter-Ammergau, and the surrounding country, and the next day, Sunday, they are all to meet here for a great thanksgiving. The following Sunday will be the festival of the Geistlicher Rath. One sees how much of the happiness of the people is bound up with their church life.

THE HOUSE OF JACOB HETT ("PETRUS")

VIII.

THE KING AND THE PLAYERS.

There was great commotion in the village two days ago. After the King had attended the last performance of the Passion Play, and had returned to the Linderhof, he sent to the burgomaster an invitation for ten of the principal players to dine at his hunting villa that evening. At the same time he sent a present of a thousand guldens to the village, with the command, that it should to devoted to a benevolent purpose. Everybody was in a flutter of excitement when the King's messenger arrived, and with him the five carriages, to convey the chosen ones to the Linderhof. It was then arranged that the following players should represent the community before his Majesty: Joseph Maier (Christus), Jacob Hett (Petrus), Johannes Zwink (St. John), Johann Lang (Caiaphas), Gregor Stadler (Annas), Gregor Lechner (Judas), Johann Diemer (the Choragus), Tobias Flunger (Pilatus), Franziska Flunger (the Virgin), Josepha Lang (Mary Magdalene). Francie, always simple and natural, wore her usual quiet dress; but it was a pity to see the men, who look so extremely well in their costumes, disfigured by the tight, old-fashioned black coats and hats, kept for grand occasions. Flunger alone wore his peasant dress, and preserved his dignified appearance.

It was ten o'clock on a lovely moonlight night when the players returned, in the same carriages that had been sent for them. Each of them in turn, beginning with the "Mary," had ten minutes audience with the King, who expressed himself deeply impressed and touched by the Play, and said that, as long as he lived,

73

he could never lose the remembrance of it. Francie and her father never tired of speaking of the grand repast that was served to them, with red wine, and champagne and cigars. All returned home with hearts full of grateful feeling towards their King. The young monarch addressed Francie, and praised her for her conception of the difficult part of the "Virgin," which, he said, she had acted out with graceful ease and naturalness. He spoke of Schauer, the "Christus" of 1860, whose life in Munich, after becoming inflated with success, was well known to him.* Some of the men went through the ordeal of the audience with great calmness. Others were too excited to preserve their natural manner and ease.

Nellie has just come in from the village, and wishes to take my pen, in order to write something that Frau Lechner has told her about the great reception at the Linderhof: —This morning I went to finish my study of Frau Lechner's kitchen, and she told me all about the audience her husband had with the King. On Monday the King came to see the play, attended by a prince of the house of Hesse, and in great style, his carriage drawn by four splendid horses. "The King" said Frau Lechner, "looked neither to the right nor to the left, but sat quite steady all the time of the performance, and was very deep in his thoughts. He drove away amidst the cheering of the people, and looked very handsome, as he acknowledged their greetings. He was so pleased, that the next day he sent a messenger to invite ten of those who took the principal parts, to the Linderhof, among the mountains. My husband was one of the favored ones. The King talked for fifteen minutes with him, and asked him, if the part he took was not one of the most difficult? Then he asked him, if he was married. He told him he had married twice, and that he had one little boy. Does he take part in the play? asked the King. Yes, he is one of the genii. What costume does he wear? And when he heard what it was, he said, Yes, I remember him, and spoke much more, that my husband did

---

* The villagers are proud of the fact that the passion play was created by simple villagers, and they are not pleased when a person tries to capitalize on his temporary fame.

not tell me. He gave them a good feast, and when they had finished, bid them take what they could not eat home to their wives and children, as a greeting from him. He asked, too, if our little boy was among the children who came to Grasswang to meet him, and sang: Long live the King. He sent the head-forester's wife a great basket of flowers, and in the midst of them she found a splendid set of jewelry."

Just as Frau Lechner was telling me this, Herr Lechner came in, and told me much of interest. "First of all" he said, "we were shown the dining-room, but seeing the many beautiful silver things, bouquets, and other ornaments on the table, we thought all this was merely to look at; but we found that all the viands had to be eaten! When the King called me in to the audience, I had a very strange feeling about the heart. But his majesty was very cordial, and when he addressed me, 'Ah, Judas!' I felt at once at my ease, and we talked together just like two old friends. He praised the performance very much, and then said to me: 'Judas, your part is one of the most difficult'—'and thankless' I said. —'To the crowd,' answered, the high-minded young King, pointing downwards; and then putting his hand to his breast, added, 'Not to me; I appreciate it.' 'Tell me, Judas,' he continued, 'what kind of a feeling have you when you find yourself entirely alone on the stage? Do you not fear?'" Lechner told him that he did, years ago, but now no more. He was evidently very proud of what the King had said, and I too rejoiced with him that he had found such appreciation.

But I must not forget the account of the dinner, that Judas has just told me. While they were dining, the King mounted his horse for a ride, leaving the players to enjoy the meal alone. After a while a valet entered the room, and informed them, that his Majesty would soon return, and would enter the room through the northern door. "May we bring out a toast to his Majesty?" they asked. "It will certainly please him," replied the valet; and so, when the King stepped in the doorway, riding-whip in hand, he was greeted with three cheers, and with two strophes of the Bavarian national hymn, in beautiful harmony. The King bowed his

thanks, "and" adds Judas, "his heart was won." He ordered all the rooms to be opened for the inspection of his "dear Ammergauers" as he called them, wound two bouquets with his own hands for the "Mary" and the "Magdalene," ordered a stock of cigars for the men, and had them entertained for more than four hours, starting for Schloss Berg,* on the Lake of Starnberg, at eight o'clock at night. In the annals of Ammergau, this day will be marked as the most eventful of all days in the history of the Passion Play. It rewards the people for all the devotedness which they have shown throughout the entire summer. They would have been much disappointed, if the King had never attended the play, and I am very glad he came, as he is a true lover of dramatic art in its purer forms. He has promised the villagers to attend the performance of some of their secular plays, such as the "Founding of the Monastery of Ettal" or "Otto von Wittelsbach," and wishes them to build a new rehearsal theatre, as soon as possible. He is also going to have a beautiful marble cross planted on an elevation near the village, with Christ nailed to it, and John and Mary standing at the foot.† He also wants to have all the scenes and tableaux of the Passion Play photographed, and has commanded his court photographer, Herr Albert, of Munich, to come to Ammergau at once for that purpose.‡

Extract from Nora's Note Book. — The photographers of the King are at work. Just now it was drummed out, that all the men, women and children having any connection with the play should come to the theatre immediately. Little Johanna, Maier's eldest child, came up to show us the pretty dress she wears in one of the tableaux. I asked her what she played, and the little thing put up her finger, and turned her head on one side, saying: "So!" Nellie

---

* Berg Palace was a favorite residence of Ludwig II's. It was there that he died, allegedly of accidental drowning, in 1886.

† The twenty-ton monument was completed in 1875 and hauled with great difficulty (and the loss of two lives) up to its position overlooking Oberammergau on one of the foothills of the Kofel, where it remains today.

‡ Joseph Albert published the photos in a limited edition in 1873.

and I have been living in Frau Maier's rooms for a fortnight past, as some friends we love very much have arrived from America, and occupy our old quarters. It was sad enough here last week, for the baby of six months' old was taken ill on Sunday, and on Monday became so much worse, that they saw it could not recover. On the day of the King's visit, the afflicted father had to leave the little one he loved best, knowing it was dying. His last words were, "God grant that she may live till I come home." But she did not, and his wife had a sorrowful greeting for him when he returned. I had to leave the room, when I saw the great grief of the strong man, who was trying all the time to calm his wife, but would take no comfort himself. Yesterday the child was buried. The priest was preceded by the acolytes and a little boy carrying the wooden cross, on which was carved the baby's name and age, and which was to be placed at the head of the grave. Immediately after the priest came a very young girl, dressed as a bride, only that her wreath was of white roses. In her arms she carried the tiny coffin, all covered with white flowers. Then followed the father, who held his other little child by the hand. When they reached the grave, two kind looking women came and took the coffin, and lowered it, oh, so tenderly into its last resting-place. Things have now been put in their places again in the house, and the little cradle is carried up to the garret; but still the mother frequently starts, and exclaims, "Oh! if it were only true, that I hear my Rosa's cry for me! But I hear it so plainly, and know it is nothing, but my own thoughts. Oh! it is so hard to bear, for I cannot still her when she cries."

The marriage of Maier's brother has just taken place. A wedding feast generally lasts two days, but this was not a very fine one. We went to the church, though it rained hard. First there was music, then a kindly address by the priest to the pair standing all alone. The father of the bride and the brother of the bridegroom had seats in the pews on either side, while the bridesmaids were in the front pews, behind two groups of little children. The putting on of the ring was followed by the priest taking from his neck a golden band, lined with crimson, and binding together the right hand of each. Then came the mass, well sung, and very pleasing;

and at the end of all, a goblet of wine was held by the priest, first
to the lips of the bridegroom, then to those of the bride, and then
to each of the immediate friends. The priest gave his blessing, and
left the church, followed by most of the people, while the married
couple still knelt before the altar. The bride was certainly the more
devout of the two, for her husband, having finished his prayers,
stood up, wiped the dust from his knees, then from his hat, and
stood looking at her, as if wondering when she would be ready.
At last he started off alone, whereupon she crossed herself rapidly, arose, and followed him. The wedding feast was at the old
Post Inn, and when Maier came home this evening, he said they
were all dancing there. "Herr Maier, why don't you dance, too?" I
asked. "Oh, I am no friend of dancing," he replied, "I would much
rather come home, take off my boots, and make myself and my
wife comfortable. I am no longer a man of the world. I must go
again to-night, because I belong to the family; but it is no pleasure
to me; and I wish it were over. On my wedding day we came quietly
home, and had our dinner just as if nothing had happened; and were
much happier than if we had danced, and drunk beer." "Why did or
do you not go, Frau Maier?" I enquired. "I am in mourning, dear
Fräulein." "And is not your husband the same?" "No" she said,
"for so young a child only the mother mourns with us."

Extract from Nellie's Note Book. — Nora and I are still at Maier's
house, and being nearer the theatre than when at Flunger's, we take
every opportunity of going there, to see the photographers at work.
The rainy season has really set in. This morning, cold and fresh,
we went with mother and "Petrus," and a crowd of folks all dressed
for the "Entry into Jerusalem." How really oriental it seemed! The
grouping and the harmony of colour, —all crudeness toned down
by the exposure through the summer, —are quite wonderful. It is
a difficult picture, and they try it three times. Even into this hard
work the people carry their earnestness. How bitterly cold it is
for Maier and the two thieves in the "Crucifixion" scene! The children in groups around are as still as death. I do not lose my impression of the grandeur of the scene, even when the only sound

is the monotonous voice of the photographer, as he counts the time for the pictures. Great as is the desire of the people to finish and be at rest, there was quite an excitement when the photographers wished to continue their work on Sunday, and their doing so was immediately forbidden by the priest, for there is a very careful observance here of the Sabbath day.

THE HOUSE OF "LAZARUS" AND THE "SCRIBE"

IX.

A PASSION SERMON.

I write in the churchyard. Yesterday was cold, sad, and stormy. The Passion Play at last over, I had a painful feeling of loneliness, a questioning wonder, as to how I should find the villagers in their ordinary life, and without any weekly excitement to look forward to. To-day the sun shines warm and bright on the old wall where I rest and write, and my questioning is at an end, for I have been with the people at their prayer, and feel how genuine is their piety. May our Father in Heaven bless this little spot!

There was a special service this morning, at the burial of a young maiden, who was to have been married in three weeks. All the church was in soft shadow, but just where the school children sat, under the east window, the light fell on their uncovered heads and clasped hands, and a lovely group they made, and full of promise for coming years, the girls so neat and modest, the boys so handsome and brave-looking. I watched the congregation pass out: first the boys and girls, with the teacher at their head, then the grown people, and last of all the mourners, in their costumes, the women wearing great fur head-dresses, the men old fashioned coats with tight sleeves, and cylinder hats of long ago. There was perfect quiet in the church all the time of the service. People did not pass in and out, as in other places, but waited reverently for the blessing of the aged priest, so honored and beloved. Many waited outside the gate to speak to him; and the children, even the toddling wee things, ran to meet him.

When I returned home, I was fortunate enough to find in the library of Flunger's large guest-chamber, a printed copy of one of the Geistlicher Rath's sermons to his congregation, composed just before the first performance of the Passion Play in the year 1850. It is a very remarkable effort, because of its perfect freedom from all confessional acrimony. Indeed, I am so pleased with it, that I have had it translated, because it gives such a deep insight into the relation of the aged pastor to his flock. The title is: "Words of Admonition, by Pfarrer G. Alois Daisenberger,* addressed, on the day before the first performance of the Passion Play, to the Community of Ober-Ammergau, in the year 1850." The text is taken from the Gospel of St. John, XIV. 27. "Peace I leave with you; my peace, I give unto you, not as the world giveth give I unto you." At the commencement he asks the question: "What effect should the representation of the Passion Play produce upon our community?" He answers it in the following words:—

Devout Hearers! On the festival of Pentecost, Our Lord completed in the Apostles the work of grace which during the course of three years he had been instilling into their hearts. The very first sight of the Divine Teacher had made so deep an impression upon them, that they had immediately believed in Him, and had followed Him. During the three years that they lived with Him, the unspeakable love of their Teacher and Master, and His miraculous deeds, strengthened their faith more and more. This faith was, indeed, somewhat shaken by the fearful events of the captivity, sentencing and crucifixion of the Lord; but it was revived and gained new power, and became unshakable, when they met again their Risen

---

* Daisenberger revised the play text written by Dr. Othmar Weis, 1769–1843, a priest at Ettal. The first production of the play under his leadership was in 1850. He continued as *Spielleiter,* or play director, through the 1870/71 season. He published a history of the village, *Geschichte des Dorfes Oberammergau,* in the *Oberbayerisches Archiv für vaterländische Geschichte* (Munich, 1859–61). It was reprinted with an introduction by Helmut W. Klinner (Oberammergau, 1988).

Saviour, and saw Him ascend into heaven. Then was fulfilled the promise of Him who had gone home to the Father! By the descent of the Holy Ghost, the disciples were filled with light from above, and fitted out with courage from heaven not merely to be firm in the faith themselves, but to bear this faith unto all nations, and to communicate their conviction victoriously to the Jews and to the heathen. O, may the faith proceeding from the Father and from Christ, the Spirit of Light and Power, which lived and worked in the disciples of our Lord after that festival of Whitsuntide, also inspire us all! May it confirm this whole community, not merely in the living faith in Christ, and in His divine teachings; but also enlighten and strengthen all, so that they glorify the name of Jesus the Crucified, and invite thousands of their fellow-men to the perfect love of Him.

"O, my dear friends! Our community has this year to fulfil a great and sacred mission. It has, to a certain degree, to take part in the apostolic office. After the Day of Pentecost, the Apostles went out among men, and preached of Christ the Crucified; they announced His doctrines and deeds, His sufferings and death, His resurrection and glorification, showing that in Him the sayings of the ancient prophets, in Him the types of the Old Testament, had found fulfilment; and that through Him and none other could salvation be obtained. As to us, we do not go out into the world to proclaim the name of the Crucified One; but in the course of the summer thousands will come to us, the pious and the luke-warm in faith, the believers and the unbelievers; and it will be for us to represent to these thousands, from far and near, the same things which the Apostles preached, namely, the sacred doctrines of the Divine Teacher, the grandest examples of His love, His bitter sufferings, His sacrificial death for humanity, His glorious victory over death and hell, the prophesies and types of the Old Testament fulfilled in Him. If we work together in holy zeal, determining to exhibit these scenes in a worthy manner, then with the grace of God there can proceed from this community great blessings to our fellow men. Through the living remembrance of the Saviour's death for our sakes, many pious Christians will be moved and edi-

fied in faith, will be strengthened in love, and will return home
with renewed determination to remain true followers of Christ!
Many, even of the lukewarm and the light-minded, will not be
able to dissipate all the earnest impressions of what they see and
hear; and these impressions may become in them the seed-corn
of a zealous Christian life! The sight of the human nature of the
Redeemer, of the bitter torments which he bore for the sake of
sinners, may perhaps call forth tears of penitence from many a
hardened one; and with God's grace these tears may be the
foreboders of an earnest conversion; and the witnessing of the
Passion may become the way by which the Good Shepherd seeks
and finds the lost lambs of the flock. And who knows if not here
and there, some one, led hither as to a secular play by curiosity, or
by the desire of being pleased, or, indeed coming with the intention of laughing at the representation together with its defects in
form and execution, —if not, I say, here and there such a one will
depart with totally different thoughts from those with which he
came; at least something will cling to his soul which, after a space
of years, may germinate and aid in the transformation of his inner life?

"But, beloved friends, God's pleasure and God's blessing
will only then accompany our work, if we undertake it with pure
intentions and holy zeal. Oh, my dear friends, if selfish reasons, if
the mere desire of fame and gain were to inspire our actions, no
blessing will rest upon them. In such a case God would look down
upon us in displeasure, and our work would then be an abuse, de-
grading to the Most High, sinful and punishable. Then we should
deserve the bitterest censure instead of fame, the severest loss instead of gain! Our forefathers vowed in times of sorrow to perform the Passion Play, with the intention of promoting thereby
the honour of God, the remembrance of the dear Redeemer, who
gave himself up to death for our sakes; as also for their edification
and that of their fellow-men. In this pious feeling, and in this only,
let us fulfil the vow of our forefathers! Let this object alone be in
our minds! Whether those who visit the representations of the
Passion Play seek anything besides Christian edification, whether

they praise or blame us, is immaterial to us; if only we ourselves and many of our fellow-men leave the Play, moved and edified, strengthened anew in true Christian sentiment, then we shall have done all that was to be accomplished. Let us not desire to shine in dramatical art, —a desire which for simple country people would be nothing better than ridiculous pride; but let the endeavor of each be to contribute as much as he can toward a representation of the Sacred History, which shall be as vivid and worthy as possible. Let us therefore begin our work with a pure intention and complete it with holy zeal!

"Each one who has to take a part in the Play, no matter what, is a necessary link in the chain. Each must be zealous to perform what is entrusted to him, to the best of his powers, and thus contribute his share to the worthy execution of the whole. You who have only to do mechanical labors, perform them with industry and attentive exactness! For you have, though unseen by man, a great task before God, no less than those who have to represent an important character in the play. You who have to represent persons who hated and persecuted the Dearest, the Most Sacred, represent those persons in their entire wickedness, hatefulness and hypocrisy, so that the spectator may be filled with abhorrence at the shameful deeds. Thereby you will contribute towards making the innocence, the gentleness, the dignity of the Redeemer appear in all the stronger light. Through the shadow in a painting the light is first made prominent! You who represent persons who ridicule and abuse Jesus, in wild brutality, let your actions be so, that the rude treatment be not exaggerated; but let it be calculated to awaken horror for the deed and sympathy for the innocent Sufferer. Thus you will serve as instruments to the glorification of Christ. You who have to represent the disciples of the Lord and the friends of Jesus, let your whole being believe and venerate the Divine Master; be attentive to his every word, and deepen your attention and gravity, when he foretells approaching events; show the most profound commiseration of spirit at his sufferings; and have brotherly love and friendliness among each other. In you, who gather about the Lord and Master, there should be found an assembly of

the best of men, the most glorious examples for all Christian communities. Thus let every one coöperate with holy zeal, so that each separate part of our work, dramatic and plastic representations, the teachings of the songs and addresses, the sweetness of verse and music, form together one harmonious whole, full of beauty and elevation. The total impression of the Passion Play will then be elevating and edifying to every spectator who brings to its witnessing an upright heart, and will serve to strengthen him in his religious feelings. Thus, what we undertake will become a truly sacred, blessed work, well-pleasing in the sight of God.

"Let us pray that the effect of the representation of the Sacred Story on the hearts of the spectators may resemble that which the Apostles, after the sending down of the Spirit, effected in the hearts of their hearers, through the announcement of the same events, eye-witnesses of which they had been. But as in ancient times the Apostles influenced men not only by their words, but also by their upright conduct, so must we, if our work is to be blessed, not only endeavor to give a worthy representation of the Most Sacred on the stage; but outside the theatre there must be exhibited Christian, moral behaviour. Neither in the scenes of the theatre, nor in the surroundings, nor in the streets, nor in the houses, nor in the church, should anything happen that would be vexatious to the visitor. No drunken persons must be seen; no enmity one against the other, no insulting speech be heard. Let every visitor find in us a truly Christian community, where Christian education and Christian feeling prevail; a community worthy to represent the most Sacred and Holy in a holy manner. . . . And, oh, if this community, through the representation of the sufferings and glorification of Christ, be strengthened in all that is good, as it was with the Apostles through the living remembrance of their Lord and Master; if this community, through the representation of the Sacred Story, glorify afar the name of the Crucified, imitating the Apostles, who glorified him among all peoples, —then hail to our community! The blessing of God will rest upon it! Our pious forefathers, they who once made the vow before God to perform the story of the Passion will rejoice in heaven. Pray

that it so be! But without God's grace the work of man is as nought. Therefore let us to-day, the day of the descent of the Holy Spirit, pray earnestly to heaven for the assistance of the Divine Spirit, in carrying out the work before us. As once over the assembly of the disciples in the hall of Jerusalem, may the Holy Spirit pour down upon this community the rich measure of His grace! Amen!"

THE HOUSE OF FRAU VEIT

X.

THE GEISTLICHER RATH.

September 29. — I have just returned from my first visit to the aged priest who has done so much for his flock, and for the improvement and success of the Passion Play. He lives in the upper story of one of the simplest houses in the village. His study-room is as unpretending as the aged man himself. It is uncarpeted, has a large Dutch stove, a sofa, a writing table, and a few relics, —that is all. Two boys were reading with him, as we entered. He raised his hand gently, and they left us. He says that he still teaches the children, with pleasure, and that their love repays him abundantly for his labor. I was glad to be able to understand all he said, while he spoke of how he came to settle down among these people, with whom he has had the closest relations for so many years. He told us how he had first written songs for the children, then composed a little poem for each, as they grew up, left the village, married, or died. After that, he began to help them to improve their great Sacred Drama, and finally to compose new religious plays for what they call their "exercise" in the intervening years. One of his best productions, "The Founding of the Monastery of Ettal," was performed before King Max, in the small rehearsal theatre of Ober-Ammergau, fifteen years ago. He has written besides, "Otto von Wittelsbach," "The Bavarians in the Peasants' War," and other pieces which he modestly entitles "Dramatic Scenes from the History of the Bavarian Fatherland." He has also written several Biblical plays, such as "The Death of Abel," "Melchisedec's Sacrifice," "Abraham's Obedience," "Judith," "Naboth"; besides dramas from the legends of "St.

Agatha" and "Genoveva." He has also arranged and added to many
of the Biblical dramas of Metastasio,* and likewise adapted for
Ammergau the tragedy of "Antigone," of Sophocles. Many of these
plays have been acted by the Ammergauers, who seem to enjoy most
the drama connected with the neighboring monastery of Ettal.

Lechner tells me that when the Geistlicher Rath first came
to Ober-Ammergau, he was frequently ill in health, but he always
thought that the performance of the secular and religious plays
by his people did him more good than all medicine. He has always directed their plays as long as he has been in the village, and
considers the village theatre, when properly directed, of great value
in the culture of his flock. All the people, men, women and children, love him, for he is untiring in looking after their welfare,
material and spiritual. When the children see him on the street,
the smallest will toddle up to him, and kiss his hand, and the aged
priest puts his hand gently upon the little head, and prays in still
for God's blessing upon it. He attended the last performance of
the play in 1871, and was deeply affected. Tears rolled down his cheeks
as he saw the well-known scenes revealed, one by one. To one of the
villagers who tried to get him to leave the theatre, fearing that the
emotion might prove too much for him, he said, "No, I would rather
remain here. It is the last Passion that I shall see in this world."

The Geistlicher Rath is one of the old school of Catholic priests which is said to be now dying out in Bavaria. He is truly
tolerant in all that he says and does, and considers us all "Christians."† In 1860, I am told, he buried two Protestants who died

* Pietro Metastasio, 1698–1782, was an Italian poet and librettist.

† Given Eliza Greatorex's strongly Protestant background, it is notewor-
thy that she finds such an ecumenical spirit in the village. Of course, the
sense of tolerance worked both ways, as many nineteenth-century Protestants held strong anti-Catholic prejudices. Even then the Oberammergau
Passion Play drew many Protestant visitors, though the village was thoroughly Roman Catholic. Only with the migration of refugees from east-
ern Europe after World War II was there a significant Protestant population in the village.

here, with Catholic ceremonies. Speaking of the school, he said to me, "The girls are at first more apt, but later the boys leave them behind in study." I asked whether that arose from the girls having more work to do at home. "No," he answered, "naturally enough they begin about fifteen to think of other things, and do not give their minds to serious study." Again, after he had thought for a few moments, he repeated, "Yes at first the girls have much more talent, but when the more earnest work begins, they fail." I said, "Many in the outside world believe that there is no evil in this village." He shook his head, and replied, "That is indeed wrong! In Ammergau they are a good people; there is no theft, no drinking, no fighting; but sin and sorrow, grief and wrong, exist here as elsewhere; and our Father in Heaven has to teach His children among the mountains, as well as in the great cities by the sea; to teach, and to forgive them also!" On the eighth of October there is to be a great festival, to celebrate the fiftieth anniversary of the old man's ordination to the priesthood. We shall remain here to see the people do him honor.

For three days men, women, and children have been bringing in birch trees and evergreens for this festival; and in the open place before the churchyard they are making miles of festoons. An avenue of young birch trees leads from the priest's house to the church, where they have erected a grand arch. Passing by the young priest's dwelling, which as well as the school-house is decorated, to the good old man's home, which they are now beginning to deck for the evening's serenade and torchlight procession, I have come to make my last sketch from near his door. It is of the church itself, his happy place of resort for twenty-six years. A gossiping crowd of women with babies stands by me, and while the men put up wreaths and festoons and gay bunches of flowers, the happy looking children shout with delight, and run to gather fresh posies, and the mothers say, "Ah! well they may, for, truly this is a priest and a father; few like him now-a-days; he helps every one, and is beloved by all!" Now they have put up the finishing decoration, with flags and inscriptions, and I do not wonder at the acclamations of the little ones, when even the good father himself

comes out to admire it. Inside the church they have collected every adornment possible. The aisles and the chancel are lined with birch trees, joined together overhead by pretty festoons of green, and the altar is splendidly arranged. I have been there often to-day, not only to see it being made so beautiful, but also to admire the handsome peasants, who are coming in crowds, and from miles around, for to-morrow's festival. At six o'clock the church was lighted, and we heard the Benedictus, the old priest officiating, and wearing pure white vestments. As I stood up to receive his blessing, it made me happy to think that his seventy-two years of life had brought him so rich a harvest of love and honor.

In the evening we were allowed to sit in his house, and wait for the torch-light procession and serenade. It came up the avenue, followed by a crowd, the musicians alternately playing and singing. After a little while the aged man came down from his room to where we were sitting, shook hands with us, his face radiant with pleasure, and then went out and stood on the steps in front, with hands folded, and eyes cast down. At the end of the serenade, a little speech was made, they gave three tremendous cheers, and the young men first pressed forward for his blessing, followed by the older ones. He spoke to them but few words, yet many even of the men were affected to tears, and the women wept outright. When it was all over, and he came into the house again, I asked for his blessing on me and mine.

Sunday Morning. — We are at the house again. Groups of little girls in white, with wreaths of orange flowers, stand near the door, next to them a crowd of young girls, with wreaths of pink and white roses, who talk merrily while they wait for the procession. The older men and women stand outside the grand arch, and the boys and young men come up with the procession, carrying flags, while cannon and music are heard in the distance. Now the bells ring out joyously. First a society bearing banners, and with uncovered heads, appears, next the chorister boys, with a magnificent mass book, and then the priests, dressed in white, and also bareheaded. All stand around the door, and when the old man comes

out, they present to him the book as a gift from his people. They hold over him a canopy, and conduct him through the long avenue of birch trees, and under the triumphal arches, over a pathway strewn with rushes and green leaves, to the church, to which we hasten; but only Nora and Walter succeed in making their way up to the choir, for the crowd is immense. It begins to rain, and we feel sorry for the people who have come from a distance and cannot get in. The procession reaches the church, the canopy is lowered, and I catch a glimpse of that quiet face, and stand listening to the music of the same mass that was composed for his inauguration, fifty years ago.

At noon the festival is over, they have brought the honored father to his home again, with great rejoicing, and Walter tells me a little of his history, alluded to in the sermon that was preached. In 1823 Joseph Alois Daisenberger was a young man, noted by his superiors as always active in his duties, and a great friend of children. In 1824 his praise still grew; in 1825 there was no better priest in the diocese; in 1834 he went as priest and school-inspector to Murnau, where he remained until 1845. In that year he came to Ammergau being then well known and beloved by the people, whose united wish it was, —a special one from the children being added, —to have him for their pastor. Here he has remained ever since, beloved and revered by every one.

Monday morning comes in with heavy rain. We sit by the window looking down sadly into our pleasant summer garden, for the last time. Yes, we must certainly go now. All is ready, and Hans with his carriage is at the door, the family crowding round with kind parting words, and Sefie bringing us the last of the autumn flowers, gathered in the rain. But it is to be only "Auf Wiedersehen," as, after the affairs of the Passion season are arranged, we hope to see many of our Ammergau friends in Munich. It is only to the village we now say "Good bye!" and very mournful and quiet it looks, as we drive away in the pelting rain. Soon it is out of sight, and at last the dear old Kofel disappears, too. And now that we have quite turned away from our mountain home, our hearts are as heavy and sad as the dreary autumn storm that comes down

upon us while our tired horses rest at the foot of the great Ettal
hill, —the same that I climbed with such eager feet, and so gay a
spirit, on that bright summer day three happy months ago. But to
comfort me comes the feeling of the better trust, the surer faith, I
bear back with me, and the thought, that if I never look again on
the homes of Ober-Ammergau, the people have made for themselves a home in my heart.

XI.

OUR SECOND VISIT TO AMMERGAU.

The coldest, saddest winter Munich has seen for many years is over. Our anticipated visit to Ammergau at Christmas had to be given up, for sickness and sorrow were with us.* And now, as I sit, and read over what I wrote last summer, I feel weary and depressed, and think that I can not finish this little work. But a happy thought comes to me: that again it is the glorious summer time; I know that the flowers are spread thickly over the meadows of the Ammer valley; I will go there, and see once more all my good friends, whose visits have been so pleasant to us through the winter. A pile of letters lies before me, and as I read some of them, my heart is warmed with sympathy. There are letters written by the daughters of Tobias Flunger, by Gregor Lechner, and by Joseph Maier. I admire the delicate handwriting of Francie and Sefie and Malie, the sweet, natural poetry of their letters to my children, and the warmth of feeling and affection their contents evince for us all. How pleasant, how refreshing these letters are!

Once, dear Sefie wrote: —"My dear Nellie: It is impossible for me to allow your birthday to pass without showing you in a few lines my deep sympathy for the occasion. You know I cannot say much, but what I do say is sincere: so I wish you all the

---

* We have no information on the problems Eliza's family faced that winter. In 1881 Eleanor (Nellie) became seriously ill when the family was in Algiers, and they had to return to New York, which must have entailed a major effort. Perhaps this was a similar situation, but not as severe.

THE HOUSE OF THE FLUNGER'S ("MARY" AND "PILATE")

happiness you are wishing for yourself, but, before everything else, health and contentment, many years of life, to the joy of your family and friends! My dear friend, we have at present as bad weather here as you have in Munich! It snows the whole day long! Perhaps you know the hopeful song: 'When it snows, when it snows, the snow-white flakes!' It has a beautiful air, which I hum all day long, as I sit and sew diligently. Sometimes I get such a longing for our summer guests." And then when Christmas came, and sickness was still with us, and we could not leave the dreary city, Francie wrote: "We hoped up to the last to see some of your dear family in our midst, to spend Christmas with us. But no one came: and I had to be content with being with you, my dear friend, in spirit. Sefie and I talk so much about you, and would often like to spend an hour with you." —Yes, I will go and see those dear people again before I leave for home!

May 30. — When I left Munich early yesterday (Wednesday) morning, for my last visit to Ammergau, the Marienplatz was filled with peasant wagons, loaded with thousands of young birch trees, for the religious festivities and solemn procession connected with the celebration of Corpus Christi. It was rumored that the King had promised to take part in the festivities, and great were therefore the expectations for the brilliancy of the occasion. Much as I should have enjoyed the gorgeous display, I was unable to wait. But I have been fully compensated for any loss of the sights in Munich, by witnessing the ceremonies connected with the day in Ober-Ammergau. At every village along the route thither, the people were busily employed in cleaning up the houses, and planting rows of young birches in the streets and before the houses, on the way to be taken by the morrow's procession.

It rained heavily as we climbed once more the steep Ettaler Berg. But were we not rewarded by that peep of Ober-Ammergau under the Kofel? —the picture that we found last year at sunset, between the burning red rowan trees, which now welcome us back with their clusters of pure white blossoms. The cow-bells rang faintly from across the fields of deep wet grass, and surely that

was our old Saturday's march we heard as we entered the village. Yes, to-morrow is the great fête of Corpus Christi in Ammergau. Our welcome to the house of the Flungers was crowded with strong remembrances of the Passion season, awakened by the music of the band, which now, without any attendant crowd of tourists, passes into the church. As we reached the house, the whole family came out to meet us. The only missing face was that of our dear girl Sefie, now away in Leipsic.* Such a noisy and happy party we were, down in the great room, all telling our experiences since last year. Francie had been for three months in Styria, in Austria, at service in a great Schloss,† but she had grown home-sick, and is now at her old work, sawing out the patterns for the wood-carving. She is looking bright and pretty, after the rest of the winter. She shows us her hard brown hands, and laughs over the work she does, but says her life is lonely without her sister. They all speak of Sefie with much love. Poor Francie's face wore a very sad expression when she was showing us her trinkets, among which was Sefie's betrothal ring. The poor child has had a most sorrowful experience! "Pilatus" himself interested me most. We seemed to have awakened him from a dream. He was eager to show us what he had done in high Art, his carvings of animals, and a tiny little picture in oils, a moonlight scene, representing a blacksmith's shop, which, he told us, he had painted during his leisure hours.

May 31. — This morning we were once more awakened by the firing of the village cannon, and the music of the village band. For the first time in many days, the sun shines brightly; and peasants clad in their picturesque costumes have come to join in the festival. The street is lined with young birch-trees, and strewn with grass and

---

* Leipzig, in the Kingdom of Saxony. Apparently she was the victim of a broken engagement.

† A castle or palace. There are many such castles or palaces in Austria, and it was not unusual for young women to spend time away from home in domestic service. See Otter Huber's mention of his mother's experience in the afterword.

wild flowers. In the church, the statues and frescoes, the bright banners and flowers, are toned together by the soft green boughs that dress the walls. All my old friends are there; and as the mass goes on, and fresh young voices join in the hymns of praise, I see them all in the same spirit of devotion as when they represented on the stage the life of the Saviour they are now worshiping. —A little later and the grand procession passed through the streets of the village and over the meadows of the valley. The children in their spotless white led the way, the young girls followed, carrying an image of the Virgin Mother, crowned with flowers, the young men bore the many-colored banners, and in the midst the Geistlicher Rath walked, while the village priest followed, bearing the Host. The procession wound slowly under the trees, across the swelling river, into the fields of flowers, and arriving on the meadow, stopped before an altar that had been erected, where the priest read a chapter from the Gospels. Again the band struck up, the maidens sang, and the old peasants followed, chanting prayers. Altogether four altars had been erected, and as the procession halted at each, it seemed only a shifting of scene from flowery meadow and mountain, to picturesque cottages and dear old homesteads. All the villagers, without a dozen exceptions, took part in the procession.

In the afternoon we paid our visits to the people. In his quiet room, with many books its best furniture, we found the beloved priest from whom I had learned the power and beauty that lie in a simple, active life of love. Joseph Maier was coming with his children down the road from his house, so we stood out in the sunlight, talking with him awhile, and I came away with my impressions of the man's earnestness of life and character deepened.

The children were singing as I passed to get my sketch of the house of Frau Veit, and I made my way into the schoolroom. The teacher was playing the violin, and beside him stood the Herr Pfarrer.* I had a good welcome when the song was over,

---

* "Mr. Pastor," the village priest who had taken over the duties of Father Daisenberger. Although Greatorex generously praises Daisenberger, she never even mentions the other priest by name.

and the teacher asked the children to sing their favorite song, "The Nightingale." I left the school quite happy for the little ones, thinking of them as I saw them in the procession of yesterday, and in the school to-day. As I came up to the smithy, and saw the groups before it, I thought of the old Dutch paintings; but as I had to make my way to the interior, in order to get the best view of my sketch, it was not quite so enjoyable; but Frau Veit helped me through my difficulty, and I was soon seated in a corner beyond the shoeing of the horses, from where I could see the little old house, into which so many thousands had pressed last year. In no other village than this could I have sat in the work-shops or in the middle of the street so undisturbed. Here I am quite at home, while beside me, the work of the smithy goes on. When the horses are shod, the smith sits on the anvil, with a pot of beer and a slice of buttered bread in his hand. Presently the children come home from school, and two pretty little ones find their way into the smithy. The grimy man drops his hammer, takes the little ones up in his arms, saying he has no children of his own, but that many come to visit him. Before I left, he brought me down a copy of Corneille* that a lady had left in his house last year, but had never written for it. Would I take it with me? he asked. I was going into the world again, and might meet the lady. He would tell me how I might know her, ——she had golden hair and blue eyes, a husband, three little children, and a black nurse!

Our last evening in Ober-Ammergau was spent in the circle of the Flunger family. We talked of old times and customs, and wondered where all the Art-treasures of Ettal had disappeared to. Flunger said that he remembered distinctly the great sale there after the secularization in the year 1803, and had in his possession a large portfolio of the Dürer engravings bought there at the time. His grandfather had told him of pictures which had been sold at

---

* Pierre Corneille, 1606–84, was a French dramatist. Of course, the village blacksmith would have no use for a book of French plays, and he naively assumed that Eliza, being an educated foreigner, would probably encounter the book's owner on her travels. See Otto Huber's references to his grandfather, the blacksmith, in the afterword.

that time for six kreuzers a piece.* Indeed, there was one in the garret which had been bought at that price: and in the dust there we found an old picture—a portrait of one of the students, in a gay costume, and sword in hand. The date is 1721. We also found a smaller picture, a Dutch landscape with figures, besides an ancient gunstock, and a number of other curiosities, all from the old monastery. When we descended to the room, we found some of our village friends waiting to bid us good-bye, some of them with specimens of their own workmanship, others with a photograph, or a bunch of Alpine roses. And now, as I write the last lines in my diary, I have said farewell, with a heart deeply moved. I will close my work with a farewell acrostic to Ober-Ammergau, which I have found in the Strangers' Book at Madame Veit's. Its author is the Rev. Vincent Eyre, of England: —

"**O** blest retreat for faith heartfelt and sound,
Banished from courts and cities! In this vale
Embosom'd, Christian piety hath found
Refuge in souls which no dark doubts assail.

Amid these mountains shines a Beacon bright,
Making the sceptic's flickering torch obscure;
Multitudes throng to hail the Heavenly light.
Earth hears once more God's wisdom from the poor!

Receive the thanks of one who hath been taught
Great truths that oft lie hidden from the wise;
Adieu! all ye who have such marvel wrought,
Until the last loud trump shall bid us rise!"

---

* When the Benedictine monastery at Ettal was forcibly dissolved and the property secularized during the Napoleonic Wars, the treasures of the institution were auctioned off.

Nachwort

Beim Betrachten der Greatorex-Zeichnungen im Jahr 2000

Otto Huber

Was die Zeiten überdauerte

Wenn ich die Zeichnungen betrachte, auf denen Mrs. Greatorex 1871 in historisch stürmischen Zeiten ein idyllisches Oberammergau liebevoll porträtierte, finde ich, der ich ein Jahrhundert später in Oberammergau aufgewachsen bin und lebe, darin nicht weniges wieder, was mir vertraut ist. Einige Häuser haben ihr Gesicht kaum verändert, z. B. „The House of the Zwinks" mit seiner Fresko- malerei, wo heute der Architekt Mayr seine Pläne zeichnet, wo ich aber auch noch den „Maler Hans", den Judas-Darsteller mit seinem Charakterkopf, Nachfahr des großen Häuserfreskanten Franz Seraph Zwink, beim Ausbessern der Fresken gesehen habe. Hier wie vor manchen anderen Häusern ist auch der Vorgarten noch da, in dem im Sommer die Rosen blühen wie eh und je, wo am Haus der wilde Wein hinaufwuchert wie einst der Krausbart im Gesicht des „Maler Hans". Daß übrigens jemand nicht nur „Zwink", sondern auch „Maler" heißt, zum Familiennamen dazu einen Hausnamen hat, ist in Oberammergau zwar nicht mehr ganz so geläufig wie früher, aber die Jüngeren haben durchaus Spaß daran, sich mit ihren uralten Hausnamen anzureden—es scheint

Afterword

Contemplating the Greatorex Drawings
in the Year 2000

Otto Huber

What Outlasts Time

When I look at the drawings in which Mrs. Greatorex lovingly portrayed an idyllic Oberammergau during the historically stormy times of 1871, I find more than a few sights familiar to me, who grew up in Oberammergau a century after her work. The facades of some houses have barely changed, such as "The House of the Zwinks" with its frescos. The architect Mayr draws his plans there nowadays, and I also saw the distinctive face of "Painter Hans," the actor who plays Judas and descendant of the great fresco painter Franz Seraph Zwink, making repairs to the frescos. The front yard is still here, just like many other houses, where the roses bloom as always and where wild grapes grow rampant up the side of the house like the curly whiskers on the face of "Painter Hans" once did. By the way, the fact that one is called not only by surname but also by a "house name"—such as the man known as "Zwink" but also as "Painter"—doesn't occur as often as it did before in Oberammergau, but the younger people have fun calling one another by their old house names—it seems

ein Teil der Rituale zu sein, die ein solches Gemeinwesen zusammenhalten.

Eines der Gebäude, die in ihren Maßen ziemlich gleich blieben und nicht ungebührlich in die Breite gingen, findet sich auch auf dem Blatt „The House of Frau Veit". Bei dem Friseur, der sich heute dort befindet, kann man sich die Haare schneiden lassen, wenn man sie sich nicht gerade, wie das hier auf offizielle gemeindliche Aufforderung hin zu geschehen hat, für das Passionsspiel wachsen läßt. Auch solch gemeinsames Haare-wachsen-Lassen gehört zu den ungewöhnlichen gemeinschaftsstiftenden Ritualen Oberammergaus.

Als kaum verändert erkenne ich auf Greatorex' Blättern auch „The House of the Flunger's" wieder, in dem einst Tobias Flunger wohnte, der Christusdarsteller von 1850, der zur Ausbildung der Bildhauer eine Zeichenschule gründete, aus der die heute überregional bedeutende Oberammergauer Schnitzschule hervorging. Tobias Flunger, dessen von einem englischen Besucher angefertigte Photographie als Christus auf dem Esel das älteste Oberammergauer Photo-Dokument darstellt, spielte im Jahr des Greatorex-Besuchs den Pilatus, seine Tochter Franziska die Maria, im Jahr 1900 findet man seine Enkelin Anna in der Rolle der Maria. Man staunt, wenn man die bescheidenen Ausmaße solcher Häuser sieht und bedenkt, was manche ihrer Bewohner zuwege brachten und mit wie wenig sie sich zufrieden gaben.

Auf der Zeichnung „The House of Lazarus and the Scribe" erkennt man das Haus, in dem heute Christian Stückl wohnt, Spielleiter von 1990 und 2000. Er muß den Kopf einziehen, der hochgewachsene Christian, wenn er bei der niederen Haustüre hineingeht. Klein auch die Fenster, wie bei vielen alten Häusern, schließlich war und ist hier in den Voralpen auf fast 900 Meter Höhe das Klima rauh, sind die Winter kalt und lang, man war also froh, wenn die Wärme des Kachelofens drinnen blieb in der Stube. Das Haus ist „eingädig"—so nannte man früher Gebäude, wo auf ein relativ niederes Erdgeschoß ein ebenfalls knapp gehaltener erster Stock aufgesetzt war. Mitte des 19. Jahrhunderts hatten hier die meisten Bewohner keine großzügigere Unterkunft. „Zum Teil an-

to be a part of the rituals that keep such a community together.

One of the buildings that have remained much the same size and have not been added on to can be found in the drawing "The House of Frau Veit." At the hair salon located there today, one can have his hair cut, if he is not letting it grow out for the Passion Play at that particular time, as has become a duty of community life here. This communal hair-growing also belongs to the unique rituals of Oberammergau.

"The House of the Flunger's" has been barely changed from Greatorex's drawings. The actor who played Christ in 1850, Tobias Flunger, lived in this house and founded an art school for sculptors, predecessor to the now renowned Oberammergauer Woodcarving School. An English visitor photographed Tobias Flunger as Christ riding the donkey, and this picture is the oldest photo document of Oberammergau. In the year that Greatorex visited the village, Flunger held the role of Pilate, while his daughter Franziska was Mary. In the year 1900, his granddaughter played Mary. It is amazing to see the modest dimensions of these houses and consider what the people accomplished and how little it took to satisfy them.

In the drawing "The House of Lazarus and the Scribe," one can see the house currently inhabited by Christian Stückl, director of the play in 1990 and 2000. Christian, who's quite tall, must duck his head to get through the low doorway of the house. The windows are likewise quite small, as in many old houses. After all, here at the foot of the Alps, 900 meters above sea level, the climate is harsh, and the winters are long and cold; so people were happy to keep the warm air from the wood-burning stove inside of the house. The house is "eingädig"—what one earlier called a building with a relatively low first floor and an equally low second floor above it. In the middle of the nineteenth century, most residents didn't have generous living arrangements. Father Daisenberger noted in 1873, "Some handsome, but mostly modest little

sehnliche, meist aber eingädige Häuschen""* notiert 1873 Pfarrer Daisenberger, der nicht nur 1860/70 den Oberammergauern den Passionsspieltext von Weis umschrieb, sondern auch eine Geschichte des Dorfes und eine Orts-beschreibung verfaßte. Wieviele Leute allerdings in solch einer kleinen Behausung Platz finden, das konnte man in den Jahren erleben, während derer Christian Stückl zur Faschingszeit seine gute Stube zum „Cafe Misthaufen" verwandelte und die Jugend des Dorfes sich um den Kachelofen drängte.

Was beispielsweise auf den Bildern fehlt

Leider hat Mrs. Greatorex uns nur Zeichnungen hinterlassen, die Oberammergau im Sommer zeigen, der schneereiche, oft strahlend herrliche Winter im Gebirge fehlt. Und sie hat sich auch mehr auf die biedermeierlichen, privaten Szenen beschränkt, auf Einzelne, die vor dem Haus arbeiten, oder kleinere Grüppchen, die am Brunnen beisammen stehen. Da fehlen z. B. die großen Feste, etwa das Fronleichnamsfest, oder auch der Fasching, den man hier hingebungsvoll feierte und immer noch feiert. Die Darstellung von Festen ließe sofort erkennen, daß die Bevölkerung damals katholisch war, während die Oberammergauer jetzt, vor allem seit Kriegsende durch die Zuwanderung protestantischer Flüchtlinge aus dem Osten, in harmonischer Ökumene leben, wobei heute sogar türkisch-stämmige Oberammergauer islamischen Glaubens bei der Passion mitspielen können.

Katholisches

Das Katholische tritt auf den Zeichnungen von Greatorex vor allem darin zutage, daß auf vielen Bildern irgendwo der Kirchturm herausschaut, der, wie es sich für einen richtigen bayerisch-barocken katholischen Kirchturm gehört, eine Zwiebelmütze aufhat. Aber Greatorex zeichnete auch das breit und solide dastehende Pfarrhaus („The Home of the Village"), das viele charaktervolle Hirten ihrer

---

* Für diesen wie für viele andere Hinweise, für großzügiges Zur-Verfügung-Stellen von Material, für Korrekturlesen und freundschaftliche Beratung gilt mein Dank dem Archivar des Oberammergauer Gemeindearchivs Herrn Helmut W. Klinner.

houses."* This man not only rewrote Othmar Weis's Passion
Play text in 1860/70 but also drafted a history of the village
and a description of the surrounding area. Just how many
people can fit into such a small dwelling? One could experience that first hand when Christian Stückl turned his living
room into "Café Misthaufen" during Carnival time and the
young people crowded together around the wood-burning
stove.

Examples of What is Missing from the Pictures

Mrs. Greatorex unfortunately left us drawings that only show
Oberammergau in the summer; the snowy, often radiantly glorious winter in the mountains is missing. She also limited her
work to private, everyday scenes with solitary people working
in front of their houses or small groups standing around by
the fountain. The great festivals—such as Corpus Christi and
Carnival, which the people devotedly celebrated and still celebrate today—are missing. The depiction of these festivals
would have shown that the population at that time was Catholic, while today people of many different denominations live
in harmony. The end of World War II brought many Protestant refugees from the East, and even those of Turkish background and Islamic belief can act in the Passion Play.

Catholicism

Catholicism is revealed in Greatorex's drawings most apparently in the church steeple looking out from many pictures—
a proper Bavarian baroque steeple with an onion dome.
Greatorex did draw the wide, solid rectory ("The Home of
the Village"), which has sheltered many a worthy shepherd
of his sheep. A few decades ago—let us lift up our complaints

---

* For this reference, as for many others, the generous supply of material, corrections, and friendly consultation on this and many other
writings, my thanks go out to the historian at the Oberammergau
Gemeindearchiv, Mr. Helmut W. Klinner.

Schafe beherbergte, aus dem man jedoch vor ein paar Jahrzehnten—
dem Herrn der Kirche sei's geklagt—ein Café gemacht hat. Eine
der Zeichnungen zeigt das Dach der spätbarocken Kirche, des
prächtigsten Oberammergauer Gebäudes, und daneben den Fried-
hof, wo man von 1634 bis 1820 die Passion gespielt hat. Auf der
Darstellung ist auch, aus dem Friedhofstor heraustretend, als
gebückter Greis Pfarrer Daisenberger zu erkennen, dem Mrs.
Greatorex voller Hochachtung ihr Buch widmete. Durch dieses
Friedhofstor treten die Kirchgänger (mag deren Zahl auch zurück-
gehen) heute wie damals, nur daß da jetzt hohe Ulmen stehen.

Ein Dornröschen-Dorf?
Daß im Vergleich zu früher heute mehr Grün vorhanden ist, das
stellt allerdings, wenn man den Greatorex-Bildern glauben darf, die
Ausnahme dar. Das Gegenteil ist meist der Fall. Wenngleich in den
letzten Jahren wieder viel dafür getan wird, den Ort grün aufzu-
rüsten, sind doch nicht wenige schöne Bäume dem Moloch Verkehr
oder der allzu praktischen Gesinnung eines Hausherrn zum Opfer
gefallen. Auf den Greatorex-Zeichnungen aber sprießen die Bäume,
die Büsche. Manche der Häuser sind wie Dornröschen-Schlösser einge-
wachsen in die Natur. Dazu mag wohl die mit romantischer Land-
schaftsmalerei wie mit englischer Gartenkunst vertraute Zeichnerin
ein wenig hinzugetan haben, ein bißchen Traum vom natur-
verbundenen Leben, wie ihn neben dem nach Tahiti auswandernden
Gauguin viele zivilisationsverdrossene Stadtleute träumten.
    Die Häuser wirken selbst wie ein Stück Natur. Das liegt
zum Teil daran, daß nur alte Gebäude abgebildet sind, in die sich, wie
in ein altes Gesicht, das Leben eingeschrieben hat (im Gegensatz zu
der Tatsache, daß in der 2. Hälfte des 19. Jahrhunderts manches Haus
neu gebaut wurde, weil die Bevölkerung anwuchs). Ein zweiter Grund
ist, daß die Zeichnerin vor allem die zwar nicht ganz ärmlichen,
aber doch bescheidenen Behausungen auswählte, in denen Darsteller
der Passion wohnten, hingegen die wenn auch nicht zahlreichen,
so doch vorhandenen stattlichen Gebäude beiseite ließ, wie sie vor
allem die Handeltreibenden, die Schnitzwaren-Verleger, besaßen.
    Was aber die Häuser auf den Zeichnungen so nach Natur

to the Lord—it was made into a café. One drawing shows the roof of the late-baroque church, the most magnificent building in Oberammergau. Next to it is the cemetery, where the Passion Play was held from 1634 to 1820. Father Daisenberger, to whom Mrs. Greatorex dedicated her book with deepest respect, can be recognized in the picture as a bent old man coming out of the cemetery gate. Churchgoers make their way through this same gate today as they did then (though their number today is less); only now tall elms line the way.

A Sleeping Beauty Village?

There is more greenery today than previously—based on the Greatorex drawings—which is unusual. The opposite is usually the case. Though much planting has been done recently to add greenery, more than a few lovely trees have been sacrificed for the sake of implacable traffic or the all-too practical concerns of a homeowner. The trees and bushes are sprouting in Greatorex's drawings. Many of the houses have, like Sleeping Beauty castles, grown into nature. And then the artist, who was familiar with romantic landscapes and English gardening, art, may have added a little—the dream of a life in tune with nature, just as the city people, fed up with civilization, dream of.

The houses themselves are right out of nature. This is partly due to the fact that only old houses are portrayed, in which life has left its mark, as it does on an old face (in contrast to the fact that in the second half of the nineteenth century, many a new house was built to house the growing population). A second reason is that the artist chose to draw the homes of the Passion Play actors, which, although not poor, were still relatively modest. She left out the impressive buildings which existed, even if small in number, probably because they housed the people in trade, the great merchants of woodcarvings.

What makes the houses she drew seem so true to

ausschauen läßt, ist wesentlich das heute noch reichlich und wieder
in steigendem Maß beim Hausbau verwendete Holz, dieses nicht
zu bändigende organische Material, das nie ganz zur Ruhe kommt,
das schrumpft, sich dehnt, reißt, sich verbiegt, sich dunkel oder
silbrig, braun oder rot gefärbt, ein Material, das sich auch leicht
ausbessern läßt, so daß manche Häuser wie alte Hosen ausschauen,
geflickt und wieder geflickt. Meist besteht da nur das Erdgeschoß
aus Mauerwerk, während das Obergeschoß aus Holz errichtet ist,
in der für das Alpengebiet typischen Blockbauweise. Holzverkleidet
auch die Tennen, der Aufbewahrungsort für das Heu über dem
Stall, zu dem man über eine Tennenbrücke hinaufkommt, wie sie
auf dem Bild „The House of Jacob Hett" abgebildet ist. Balkone
sieht man zwar weniger als heute, aber dem einen oder anderen
Haus war—wie man auf der Zeichnung „View from the House
of Caiaphas" feststellen kann—eine gitterartige Holzkonstruktion,
eine sogenannte „Laube" vorgehängt, geeignet zum Trocknen und
Dörren. Oder es gab auch, wie die gleiche Darstellung zeigt, von
hölzernen Balken gestützte Arkadengänge.

Aus Holz natürlich auch die weit vorkragenden Vordächer,
ähnlich breiten Hutkrempen, die verhindern, daß es einem bei Schnee-
fall ins Gesicht schneit. Kunstvolle Verbindungen der Balken finden
sich in den Giebeldreiecken darunter, sogenanntes „Bundwerk", oft
ausgeziert mit urtümlich-magischen Motiven. Schließlich fertigte
man die Dächer selbst aus Holz, deckte die Häuser mit hölzernen
Legschindeln. Zwar waren deren Herstellung und das Eindecken
extrem arbeitsintensiv, aber die aufgewendete Zeit galt nichts und
das Material war billiger als die gebrannten Dachziegel. Damit die
Schindeln aber nicht vom Sturm davongeblasen werden konnten,
wurden sie mit Steinen beschwert. Auch dies—die steinbeschwerten
Dächer vor dem Hintergrund schroffer Felsen—trägt wieder bei
zu dem Gefühl des Eingebundenseins der Häuser in die Natur.

Was man außerdem aus dem Rohstoff der Wälder machte

Wer die Bedeutung dieses in den Wäldern rings um Oberammergau
reichlich nachwachsenden Rohstoffes Holz für die Oberammergauer damals ermessen möchte, der müßte allerdings in die Häuser

nature is essentially the abundant amount of wood, which to-
day is again being used in increasing quantities. This untamable
organic material never really comes to rest; it shortens and
lengthens, cracks, bends, turns darker or more silver, brown
or more red in tone. It is a material that can easily be easily
mended, so that many houses have begun to look like old trou-
sers, patched and patched yet again. Most houses have only a
ground floor of masonry, while the upper level is made of
wood, typical for the building style of the Alps region. The
haylofts above the stable are also sheathed in wood. One
reaches the loft via a bridge, just as it is illustrated in the picture "The House of Jacob Hett." Balconies were not as preva-
lent as they are today, but the occasional house—as one can
see in the drawing "View from the House of 'Caiaphas'"—
had a bar-like wood construction, like a trellis, made for dry-
ing clothes and food, hung onto it. Also apparent from this
drawing is the occasional arcaded walkway supported by
wooden beams.

　　Also made out of wood, or course, are the jutting
eaves, like wide hat brims, to keep the snow from falling on one's
face. Artistically crafted joints between the beams called "Bundwerk" can be found under the gable triangle and are often
elaborately decorated with magical, archaic motifs. Finally, even
the roofs were finished with wood and the houses covered with
shingles. Producing the materials and shingling the house were
extremely labor-intensive, but the time spent didn't matter
much, and the material was less expensive than the fired roofing
tiles sometimes used. The shingles were weighed down with rocks
to prevent them from being blown off in a storm. These rock-
weighted roofs, coupled with a backdrop of steep cliffs, contribute to the feeling of the integration of house and nature.

Using the Raw Material of the Forests

To appreciate the meaning that this abundantly growing raw
material has for the villagers, one needs look into the houses
that Greatorex drew. She certainly saw the sawing, planing,

hineinschauen, die Greatorex gezeichnet hat. Sicherlich hat auch
sie gesehen, wie da gesägt, gehobelt, geschnitzt, gedrechselt wurde,
wie Puppenköpfe und anderes Kinderspielzeug entstanden,
Kruzifixe, Heiligenfiguren, vielerlei Gegenstände frommer Andacht
oder auch kleine Dinge zur Verschönerung des bürgerlichen Haus-
halts wie Behältnisse für Uhren. 62 Schnitzer gab es hier, 4 Faßmaler
(Bemaler von Schnitzwerken), 3 Drechsler, 7 Schreiner, 48 Klein-
häusler, die als Waldarbeiter ihr Brot verdienten, und 18 Landwirte,
die von ihrer Landwirtschaft nur leben konnten, wenn sie durch
Holzhandel und Lohnfuhrwerk dazuverdienten.

Auch Oberammergauer bleiben nicht immer zu Hause

Es gab aber zudem auch diejenigen, die, um das hier Produzierte
zu verkaufen, in die große weite Welt ziehen mußten. So handelte
Peter Rendl, der Johannes-Darsteller von 1890 und 1900, zwischen
diesen Spielen mit Schnitzwaren in London, und der wohl-
habendste Oberammergauer, der Schnitzwarenverleger Guido Lang,
arbeitete von 1874–76 bei seinem älteren Bruder Hugo in Liverpool,
der dort eine eigene Firma für Schnitzereien aufgebaut hatte.

Europaweit boten die Oberammergauer ihre Waren zum
Verkauf an, von Sankt Petersburg bis Neapel, von Holland bis hinunter nach Spanien. Und sie waren stolz auf diese Weltläufigkeit.
Als der Kurfürst 1770 alle bayerischen Passionsspiele verbieten ließ,
betonten sie in ihrer Bittschrift, daß die Hauptrollen von Männern
gespielt würden, „welche halb oder ganz Europa bereist haben, mit-
hin wohl zu unterscheiden wissen, was an anderen Orten für einfältig
und verwerflich gehalten wird und was bei einer so heiligen Vorstel-
lung gangbar ist". Im übrigen war es in bürgerlichen Oberammergauer Familien, die größere Pensionen betrieben, durchaus üblich,
daß man Mädchen, wie z. B. auch meine Mutter, für ein Jahr in
die Dienste einer englischen Familie gab, damit sie gutes Englisch
lernten.

Die Heimat und der Blick nach draußen

Da kommt eine eigene Spannung in den Blick, die das Oberammergauer Leben über Jahrhunderte bestimmte und irgendwie noch

carving, and turning that were done there, how doll heads and other children's toys, crucifixes, figurines of saints and other objects of piety were created—even small items for prettying up the bourgeois home, such as clock cases. Sixty-two carvers lived here, along with four painters (artists who paint wood-carving), three turners, seven joiners, forty-eight cottagers, who earned their bread working in the forests, and eighteen farmers, who could subsist from what they grew if they supplemented their income with peddling wood and hauling.

Even Oberammergauers Don't Always Stay Home

In addition, there were those who had to venture out into the world to sell the goods produced in Oberammergau. Peter Rendl, the actor who played John from 1890 and 1900, did business between play seasons selling wood carvings in London. The most well-to-do man from Oberammergau, the carving merchant Guido Lang, worked from 1874 to 1876 in Liverpool with his older brother Hugo, who had built up his own company for wood carvings there.

The Oberammergauer offered their goods for sale all over Europe, from St. Petersburg to Naples, from Holland to Spain. They were proud of their globetrotter ways. When the prince elector forbad all Bavarian passion plays in 1770, the citizens of Oberammergau submitted a petition stating that the lead roles of the play were played by men "who have traveled around part or all of Europe and are in the position to decide if something would be seen as simple-minded and reprehensible in other regions and what is permissible in such a holy production." It was also typical in the middle-class Oberammergau family that did a fair business taking in boarders that the girls—my mother, for example—went to be servants in an English household to learn good English.

Homeland and the View to the Outside World

There is a peculiar tension that has determined the life in Oberammergau for centuries and in some ways determines it

heute bestimmt. Einerseits lag dieses Voralpental geographisch im Abseits, was die Herausbildung einer Eigenkultur förderte, zu der politisch auch die spezielle jahrhundertelange Anbindung an das benachbarte Benediktinerkloster Ettal beitrug. Doch das bedeutet nicht, wie manche irrtümlich meinen, daß der Ort—ähnlich einem hinter sieben Hügeln versteckten Schneewittchen-Land—von der allgemeinen Entwicklung abgeschnitten gewesen wäre oder daß man ihn sich heute noch als eine Art bayerischen Urwald vorstellen dürfte, zu dem die Strahlen der Zivilisation kaum hinfinden. Ein wenig schwingt eine derartige Sicht ja auch in Greatorex' Zeichnungen hinein, z. B. im Fall des „Going into Oberammergau", wo sich die Kutsche dem Dorf recht abenteuerlich auf unwegsamem Gelände zu nähern scheint.

Denn da gibt es auch die andere Seite, daß nämlich dieser von Greatorex gezeichnete holprige Pfad identisch ist mit einer seit vorrömischer Zeit bedeutenden Verkehrsader und daß Oberammergau an dieser Nord-Süd-Route lag, die Italien, d. h. den Kulturraum des Mittelmeers, mit dem deutschen Kultur- und Wirtschaftsraum verband. Über diese Verkehrsader kamen Römer nach Germanien, zogen Kaiser, aber auch zahllose Pilger hinunter nach Rom. Lange war Oberammergau eine Handelsstation auf der Strecke zwischen den Kulturhauptstädten Venedig und Augsburg. Da gingen nicht nur Waren in die eine und die andere Richtung, sondern auch Informationen, Wissen, so daß man durch die Anbindung an diesen Verkehrsweg auch an dem aktuellen geistigen Austausch partizipierte. Nicht untypisch ist deshalb, daß ein Oberammergauer, Adam von Ammergau, im Italien des 15. Jahrhunderts zu einem der frühesten europäischen Inkunabeldrucker wurde, ein anderer zu den ersten Studenten der neugegründeten Ingolstädter Universität gehörte.

Hinaus in die Ferne

Daß die Oberammergauer häufig nach draußen gingen, hatte seinen Grund auch in ökonomischen Zwängen. Die Voraussetzungen für die Landwirtschaft waren hier denkbar ungünstig: Zum rauhen Klima kamen fast jährliche Überschwemmungen hinzu, die Böden waren von Haus aus mager, das landwirtschaftlich nutzbare Terrain sehr begrenzt. So gab es manche, die wegzogen, und andere,

yet today. On the one hand, this Alpine valley lies out of the way geographically, furthering its development as a unique culture, to which the village's special centuries-long connection to the neighboring Benedictine monastery in Ettal politically contributed. This does not mean, as some falsely believe, that the area had been cut off from all progress, like a fairy tale land hidden behind seven hills, or that one can picture it as a sort of Bavarian primeval forest, scarcely touched by the shining light of civilization. A little of this view has slipped into Greatorex' drawings, such as in "Going in to Oberammergau," where the carriage appears to be approaching the village via difficult terrain—a downright adventurous journey.

On the other hand, Greatorex drew a bumpy path that is identical to an important thoroughfare from pre-Roman times, and Oberammergau was located on the north-south route that connected Italy—that is, the culture of the Mediterranean—and the business and cultural regions of Germany. Romans came to Germania via this thoroughfare, and emperors and countless pilgrims tramped it on their way to Rome. For a long time Oberammergau was a trade station on the route between the cultural capitals of Venice and Augsburg. Not only did goods travel in either direction on this route, but also information and knowledge, so that one took part in the most current exchanges of thinking thanks to this location. It is therefore not extraordinary that one villager, Adam of Ammergau, was one of the earliest European printers, in Italy in the fifteenth century, and that another was one of the first students at the newly founded Ingolstadt University.

Into the Far and Wide

The travels of the Oberammergauers can be attributed to economic need, which often brought the Oberammergauers out of their homeland. Agricultural conditions here were less than ideal: in addition to the harsh climate, there were floods almost annually, the soil was poor, and the agriculturally useful terrain was very limited. So there were some who moved

die sich nach dem Prinzip „Not macht erfinderisch" etwas einfallen
lassen mußten, was sie mit den vorgefundenen Rohstoffen anfangen
konnten. Sie wandten sich—vielleicht nicht unbeeinflußt von den
nahegelegenen Klöstern Ettal und Rottenbuch—dem Kunsthand-
werk zu, vor allem der Schnitzkunst, die sich hier schon im 15. Jahrhundert nachweisen läßt. Die Notwendigkeit, ihre Produkte zu
verkaufen, mußte aber auch sie den Blick nach außen richten lassen.

Der damals die Außenorientierung erleichternde An-
schluß an die Nord-Süd-Verbindung war bestimmend über die
Zeiten hin. Wie stark die Ausrichtung nach Süden hin war—dem
katholischen Süden im Gegensatz zum protestantischen Norden!
—, zeigen auch Alltagsbeispiele, etwa daß mein Großvater Hugo
Rutz, der in Oberammergau Schmied war und bei der Passion 1922,
1930 und 1934 den Kaiphas und 1950 den Petrus spielte, zum Ein-
kaufen guter Kleidung nicht nach München, sondern in das öster-
reichische Innsbruck fuhr oder daß er seine Ausbildung zum
Schmiedemeister nicht in Berlin, sondern in Wien an der k.u.k.
Hofschmiede machte.

Im Grunde funktioniert diese Nord-Süd-Schiene inklusive
der Ausrichtung nach Süden noch heute. Besucher aus Übersee staunen,
wenn sie erleben, wie eng Oberammergau verbunden ist mit dieser
europäischen Koordinate. Viele wissen nicht, daß der Ort fast
unmittelbar an der österreichischen Grenze liegt, daß man mit dem
Auto in einer Stunde in Kaiserin Maria Theresias Residenzstadt
Innsbruck ist, der Olympiastadt von 1968 und 1976, in weniger als
zwei Stunden an der italienischen Grenze, daß man in drei Stunden
den Gardasee—exklusiver Ferienort schon in der römischen
Kaiserzeit—erreicht (eine Möglichkeit, die die Oberammergauer
ausgiebig nutzen) und in fünf Stunden Venedig (während man nach
Berlin acht Stunden braucht!). Und daß man natürlich—in nördlicher
Richtung—in einer knappen Stunde nach München gelangt, in die
bayerische Landeshauptstadt und internationale Kulturmetropole.

Herein in das Dorf

So leicht man aus dem Dorf in die Ferne kommt, so einfach ist es
heute umgekehrt für die Besucher von außen, nach Oberammergau

away; and others, those who lived by the principle that "necessity is the mother of invention," let an idea come to them as to what they could do with the raw materials at hand. Perhaps influenced by the nearby Ettal and Rottenbuch monasteries, they turned to artistic crafts, mostly woodcarving, of which we have evidence from as far back as the fifteenth century. The need to sell their products made them turn their sights to the outside world.

Oberammergau's location on the north-south route, which made it easier to be travel-oriented, was a deciding factor over many years. Everyday examples show how strong the orientation toward the south was—and the south was Catholic, unlike the Protestant north! My grandfather Hugo Rutz, for example, a blacksmith in Oberammergau, who played Caiaphas in 1922, 1930, and 1934 and Peter in 1922, did not go to Munich to buy good clothes, but instead to Innsbruck, and didn't train as a master blacksmith in Berlin, but rather in Vienna, at the court smithy.

By and large, this north-south route functions still today, along with its orientation toward the south. Visitors from overseas are amazed when they see just how connected Oberammergau is with this part of Europe. Many do not realize that the village is almost directly on the Austrian border and that one could be at Maria Theresa's capital, Innsbruck—the Olympic city from 1968 and 1976—in an hour by car. It's less than two hours to the Italian border, and one can also reach Lake Garda, an exclusive vacation spot already during the Roman Empire, in three hours—a proximity of which the Oberammergauers take full advantage. Venice is five hours away, but it takes eight hours to reach Berlin! Munich, the capital of Bavaria and an international cultural metropolis, is only about an hour away.

Into the Village

Conversely, it is just as easy for visitors from the outside to get to Oberammergau. This has been the case especially since

zu reisen, historisch gesehen vor allem seit 1900, als Oberammergau an das Schienennetz der Bahn angeschlossen wurde. Natürlich wurde in den vergangenen Jahrzehnten auch die durch Oberammergau gehende traditionsreiche Nord-Süd-Verbindung von Augsburg nach Garmisch verkehrstechnisch ausgebaut, doch als der Verkehr überhand nahm, führte man vor fünfzehn Jahren eine Umgehungsstraße um Oberammergau herum und unternahm manches mehr, um den Verkehr im Ort zu beruhigen und Sorge zu tragen für einen geruhsamen Aufenthalt der Gäste.

Daß der Weg nach Oberammergau von so zahlreichen Menschen genommen wurde und wird, hängt mit der im 19. Jahrhundert anwachsenden Begeisterung für die alpenländische Gebirgswelt zusammen, vor allem aber mit dem Anwachsen der Bedeutung der hiesigen Passionsspiele. Kamen um 1800 herum, wenn es gut ging, in einem Passionsspieljahr ca. 10.000 Besucher, so waren es 1850 45.000, 1860 100.000 und 1870/71 trotz der Unterbrechung durch den Krieg mit Frankreich zwischen 70.000 und 80.000. (Im 20. Jahrhundert steigerte sich die Zahl der Besucher bis zu einer halben Million!) Die begeisterten Berichte romantischer Intellektueller hatten daran ebenso Anteil wie das Bedürfnis der bedrängten katholischen Kirche nach öffentlicher Präsenz oder die verbreitete Suche nach religiöser Erfahrung in einem sich mehr und mehr säkularisierenden Zeitalter.

Die Welt kommt nach Oberammergau

Früh kamen die Zuschauer auch aus dem Ausland, schon 1850/60 besuchten einige Engländer die Spiele. Bald dokumentierte sich das übernationale Interesse auch in Publikationen. Henry Blackburn berichtete in „Art in the Mountains" (1870) von Oberammergau, 1871 erschienen die ersten englischsprachigen Veröffentlichungen zum Passionsspiel von W. S. Berry und G. C. Thomas (Philadelphia), 1860 besuchte der dänische Schriftsteller Hans Christian Andersen das Passionsspiel und publizierte 1871 in englischer Sprache seinen Bericht „Celebration at Oberammergau" (Boston). Und 1872 kam dann auch Eliza Greatorex' „The Homes of Oberammergau" heraus. Das Interesse der anglosächsischen Welt war so groß, daß Thomas Cook und Henry Gaze schon 1880 Bureaus

1900, when Oberammergau was brought into the rail network. The tradition-rich north-south route from Augsburg to Garmisch has been modernized in the last few decades, and then as traffic began to get out of hand about fifteen years ago, a bypass was built around Oberammergau. Other projects were also undertaken to decrease traffic in the village and to ensure a peaceful stay for the guests.

The fact that so many people visit Oberammergau is due to the enthusiasm for the mountain landscape of the Alps, which has been growing since the nineteenth century. But above all, it is due to the increasing significance of the Passion Play. In the 1800s about 10,000 visitors came in a Passion Play year if business was good. In 1850, 45,000 came; in 1860, 100,000; and in 1870/71, between 70,000 and 80,000 visited, despite the interruption caused by war with France. (In the twentieth century the number of visitors rose to half a million!) The enthusiastic reports from romantic intellectuals were as much a reason for this growth as the Catholic church—coming increasingly under pressure—and its need for a public presence, or a widespread search for religious experience in an increasingly secular age.

The World Comes to Oberammergau

Audiences from abroad began coming early; some English visitors attended the play as early as 1850/60. Soon international interest in the play began being documented in publications. Henry Blackburn reported about Oberammergau in *Art in the Mountains* (1870). In 1871 the first English-language publications regarding the Passion Play, by W. S. Berry and G. C. Thomas, appeared in Philadelphia. In 1860 the Danish author Hans Christian Andersen visited the Passion Play and published his English-language report, *Celebration at Oberammergau*, in Boston in 1871. Eliza Greatorex's work *The Homes of Oberammergau* came out in 1872. The interest from the Anglo-Saxon world was so great that Thomas Cook and Henry Gaze opened tourism offices in Oberammergau in 1880 and devised schemes to man-

in Oberammergau eröffneten und neue Organisationsformen ersannen, um den Besucherandrang zu bewältigen. Wie universal die Zuschauerschaft war, zeigt sich auch in Nebensächlichem, etwa darin, daß sich 1900 in den Opferstöcken der Oberammergauer Kirche Münzen aus Ägypten, Indien, Hongkong, Dollars aus USA, Mexiko, Brasilien, Bolivien und Sols aus Peru fanden. Im übrigen registrierte man sogar drei Besucher aus China.

Die Welt kam nach Oberammergau—das galt nicht nur im geographischen, sondern auch im soziologischen Sinn. Alle gesellschaftlichen Schichten versammelten sich hier. Natürlich die einfachen Leute, angefangen bei der bäuerlichen Bevölkerung der Umgebung. Aber auch und gerade die Oberschicht. Von den Repräsentanten der Gesellschaft fanden sich nicht nur die bayerischen Könige ein wie Ludwig II., sondern auch der englische Kronprinz Edward, zahlreiche Mitglieder der königlichen Familien und des Hochadels ganz Europas, dazu amerikanische Industrielle wie Rockefeller und Vanderbilt, Heroen einer neuen technischen Intelligenz wie Auguste Eiffel oder Graf Zeppelin, auch Komponisten wie Franz Liszt, Richard Wagner und Anton Bruckner, dazu Dichter, Maler, Theaterleute und vor allem zahllose Kirchenfürsten bis von New York oder Australien, darunter Kardinal Ratti, der spätere Papst Pius XI., und Nuntius Pacelli, der spätere Papst Pius XII. Es setzt einen immer wieder in Erstaunen, wieviele und wie bedeutende Menschen in dem kleinen Gebirgsdorf zusammentrafen, das zur Zeit von Greatorex nur etwa 1200 Einwohner zählte (heute ca. 5400).

Auch zwischen den Spielen

Immer größer wurde aber auch die Zahl derer, die es zwischen den Spielen nach Oberammergau zog. Mit der Entwicklung des modernen Tourismus kommen immer mehr Urlaubsuchende, die die Schönheit und den Erholungswert der Landschaft schätzen, die vielfältigen Möglichkeiten zum Wandern und Bergsteigen, im Winter zum Skilaufen auf der Piste oder in der Loipe, oder auch der Begegnung mit der Kunst der Klöster, der Rokoko-Kirchen oder der Schlösser Ludwigs II.

Dabei ergeben sich vielerlei Kontakte mit einer Bevölke-

age the throngs of visitors. The universality of the viewership coming to Oberammergau can be seen in minor details, such as the fact that in 1900 coins from Egypt, India, Hong Kong, the United States, Mexico, Brazil, Bolivia, and Peru were found in the collection plates of the Oberammergau church. Even three visitors from China were registered.

The world was coming to Oberammergau, not only in the geographic but also in the sociological sense. Every social class gathered here, naturally including the simple people, beginning with those from the local farming community, but also the upper class. Among the representatives of elegant society were not only the Bavarian kings, like Ludwig II, but also the English Crown Prince Edward, numerous members of royal families and from the aristocracy of all Europe. There were also American industrial leaders, such as Rockefeller and Vanderbilt, heroes of the new technology, such as Auguste Eiffel or Count Zeppelin, composers such as Franz Liszt, Richard Wagner, and Anton Bruckner, poets, painters, actors, and above all countless church leaders from New York to Australia, including Cardinal Ratti (later Pope Pius XI) and Nuntius Pacelli (later Pope Pius XII). It never ceases to amaze a person how many important people who came together in this small mountain village, which claimed only about 1,200 residents in Greatorex's time (today there are about 5,400).

Even Between the Plays

Ever-increasing numbers of people began coming to Oberammergau in the off season between plays. With the development of modern tourism, many more vacationers came to experience the beauty and benefits that the landscape provided—the various opportunities for hiking and mountain climbing, skiing the slopes or the cross country trails—or to enjoy to the art of the monasteries, the rococo churches, or the castles of Ludwig II.

With all these visitors, there is a great deal of con-

rung, der man nachsagt, daß sie offen und warmherzig auf Fremde zuginge. (Nicht umsonst war das zentrale Symbol der Augustiner, die Oberammergau jahrhundertelang geistlich betreuten, das brennende Herz.) Vor allem zwischen den Einzelreisenden und den privaten Vermietern entwickeln sich oft freundschaftliche, familiäre Beziehungen, wo Briefe hin und hergehen oder Gäste über Jahrzehnte hin ihre Ferien in der gleichen Pension verbringen. Auch mit den nur kurz verweilenden Passionsgästen gibt es oft lebendige Begegnungen, und mehr als ein Oberammergauer ist nach der Passion nach England oder Amerika gefahren, um dort die zu besuchen, die er ein paar Monate vorher in seinem Haus beherbergte. Selbst zu den Kurzbesuchern, die auf Oberammergau als eine der vielen Sehenswürdigkeiten der Region nur einen raschen Blick werfen, findet man manchmal Zugang, z. B. wenn man ihnen bei einer Führung Geschichte und Gegenwart des Dorfes ein wenig näherzubringen sucht.

Eine besondere Gelegenheit zu internationalen Kontakten bietet sich in Oberammergau dadurch, daß in einer 1936–38 erbauten Kaserne, mit der sich als einem Teil des Hitlerschen Aufrüstungskonzeptes wahrlich keine pazifistischen Ambitionen verbanden, nun ein Schulungszentrum der Nato untergebracht ist. Hohe Offiziere aus den Natoländern, darüber hinaus aber auch aus den assoziierten Staaten, treffen sich hier in Oberammergau im Sinn einer friedensstabilisierenden Kooperation. Manche von ihnen bleiben über einen längeren Zeitraum, und häufig entwickeln sich zwischen ihnen und Oberammergauer Bürgern lebendige Freundschaften.

Veränderungen im Alltag

Die Begegnung mit den vielen Gästen aus aller Welt läßt einen Ort selbstverständlich nicht unberührt. Am Ende des 19. Jahrhunderts resultierten daraus Veränderungen in vielen praktischen Bereichen. So wollte man—vor allem für die Gäste—mit einer zentralen Wasserversorgung und der Bereitstellung fließenden Wassers in den Haushalten den Anforderungen moderner Hygiene nachkommen und zu städtischem Konfort aufschließen. Im Sinn der Gesundheitsförderung war das sicher ein richtiger Schritt, aber es führte

tact with the villagers, who are always said to be open and warm-hearted toward those from out-of-town. (It wasn't accidental that the central symbol of the Augustinian monks, who attended to the religious needs of those in Oberammergau for centuries, was the burning heart.) Above all, a friendly, familiar relationship develops between those traveling alone and the private rent-ers, and letters are exchanged for decades to come and guests often spend their visits in the same pensions every time. There are even meaningful encounters that take place with guests who only stay for a short time to see the Passion Play, and more than one villager has traveled to England or America after the Passion Play to visit someone he or she had housed a few months earlier. Villagers find ways to interact with even those guests staying for short visits, who quickly visit Oberammergau as they take in the many points of interest in the region. A villager may meet these guests on a tour and seek to bring some of the past and present of the village to life for them.

A special opportunity to find international contact presents itself in an unlikely manner. Barracks had been built in 1936–38 as part of Hitler's armament program—hardly a peaceful project—but now are used as a schooling center for NATO. High-ranking officers, principally from the NATO states but also from other associated nations, meet here in Oberammergau with the desire to stabilize peace through co-operation. Many stationed here remain for a longer time and often develop active relationships with the citizens of Oberammergau.

Changes in Daily Life

Contact with so many visitors from all over the world cer-tainly does not leave a place untouched. By the end of the nineteenth century, this had resulted in many changes that affected various practical areas of life. On account of the guests, the town wanted to keep up with the demands for modern hygiene and for urban conveniences by providing a central water supply and running water. This was a step in

doch auch dazu, daß die meisten der zahlreichen Brunnen, die man noch auf Greatorex' Bildern sieht, abgebaut wurden und ein Stück dörflichen Lebens zu Ende ging, das Gespräch am Brunnen beim Wasserholen.

Ähnlich war wohl auch das gemeinsame Wäschewaschen am sogenannten „Mühlbach", wie es Greatorex auf der Zeichnung „Washday under the Kofel" darstellt, eine Gelegenheit sozialen Austausches. Wenngleich die Unannehmlichkeiten dieser Arbeit im kalten Wasser nicht verharmlost werden sollen, so kann man doch die ihr ein Ende setzende Erfindung der Waschmaschine auch als Verlust sehen, insofern es dadurch zu einer weiteren Privatisierung und zum Abbröckeln eines Stücks sozialen Lebens kam. Wirklich bedauernswert ist, daß man vor wenigen Jahrzehnten, auch mehr oder weniger aus hygienischen Gründen, den durch den Ort fließenden Mühlbach zuschüttete, als man den Betrieb der seine Energie nutzenden Sägemühle einstellte.

Und während auf den Zeichnungen von Greatorex die Straßen eigentlich nur wildromantische Fahrrinnen und ausgetretene Kieswege sind, mit Gräben daneben, in die das aus den Dachtraufen spritzende Wasser ablaufen konnte (siehe „View from the House of Caiaphas"), wurden in der Folgezeit die Straßen erst gepflastert, später geteert, wobei man darunter die Kanalisation anlegte. Erst im letzten Jahrzehnt baute man im Ortszentrum die so entstandenen Asphaltwüsten wieder zurück, versuchte man durch eine Pflasterung und eine Erweiterung der den Fußgängern überlassenen Flächen den dörflichen Charakter wieder zurückzugewinnen.

Manche Veränderungen ergaben sich einfach aus dem allgemeinen zivilisatorischen Wandel. So läßt der Esel, den Greatorex auf dem Blatt „The House of Joseph Mair" abbildete, nicht nur die Frage aufkommen, ob es sich da um den Passionsesel handle, der üblicherweise kein „Oberammergauer" war, sondern aus einem Dorf in der Umgebung angemietet wurde, sondern er läßt auch an die vielen Tiere denken, die früher auf Oberammergaus Straßen zu sehen waren. Da trieb man z. B. morgens die Kühe auf die Weide und abends zurück in den Stall, die dann—was durchaus erheiternd

the right direction for promoting health, but it also led to the dismantling of most of the numerous fountains that one saw in Greatorex's pictures. Part of village life thus came to an end, namely chatting at the fountain while procuring water for the day.

Similarly, the collective washing of clothes by the so-called mill stream was an opportunity for socializing, as depicted by Greatorex in "Washday under the Kofel." Although the uncomfortable nature of this work, done in cold water, should not be downplayed, one can view the invention of the washing machine as a loss insofar as it brought on further privatization and the erosion of an aspect of community life. And it's truly regrettable that the mill stream, which used to flow through the village, was filled in a few decades ago—also more or less for hygienic reasons—because the saw mill, which drew its energy from the stream, was closed.

While the streets in Greatorex's drawings appear as really only wildly romantic channels and gravel paths with ditches alongside of them for water run-off (see "View from the House of 'Caiaphas'"), these streets were later paved, then tarred, and drainage was installed underneath. Just in the last decade, the town has tried to scale back the asphalt desert that thus originated in the town center, by paving and expanding the areas for pedestrians and winning back some of its village character.

Many changes have resulted simply from the general civilizing trend. The donkey illustrated in the Greatorex drawing "The House of Joseph Mair" doesn't just make one wonder whether it's the Passion donkey—which actually was not usually an "Oberammergauer" but an animal rented from a nearby village; it also makes one think about the many animals that were found earlier on the streets of Oberammergau. For example, the cows were taken to pasture in the morning and then brought back to the stalls in the evening, and then—which was really comical—would, like their sacred Indian relatives, wend their way through the crowd, colliding with el-

sein konnte—gleich ihren heiligen indischen Verwandten durch die
Menge ziehend, mit elegant gekleideten Besuchern aus dem Passions-
theater kollidierten. Wenngleich man heute immer noch seine Milch
abends beim Bauern aus dem Kuhstall holen kann, so ist doch
gegenüber damals die Zahl der bäuerlichen Betriebe stark zurück-
gegangen, damit auch die Zahl der Kühe und ihre Präsenz im Ortsbild.
        Noch einschneidender der Verlust des Pferdefuhrwesens.
Über viele Jahrhunderte hin hatten nicht wenige Oberammergauer
von den Vorspanndiensten gelebt, die sie mit ihren Pferden bei den
Fuhrwerken leisteten, die aus dem Loisachtal über einen steilen An-
stieg in das gut 200 Meter höher gelegene Ammertal hinaufgezogen
werden mußten. Daneben wurden Pferde zahlreich in der Landwirtschaft eingesetzt. Häufig wurden sie auch Kutschen oder den sogenannten „Stellwagen" vorgespannt, einer Art Pferdeomnibussen,
die lange mit den modernen Motoromnibussen konkurrierten.
Mein Vater, der 1929 nach Oberammergau kam, kutschierte damit
z. B. Touristen von Oberammergau zum Königsschloß Linderhof,
und es gibt auch ein hübsches Photo, wo er als stolzer junger
Kutscher auf dem Bock sitzt und neben ihm, etwas verschüchtert
in Internatsuniform, meine Mutter. In den dreißiger Jahren gab er
aber typischerweise den Transport mit Pferden auf und kaufte einen
modernen, motorisierten Lastwagen. Auch mein Großvater, der
Schmied, war von solchen Entwicklungen unmittelbar betroffen.
Das Beschlagen der Pferdehufe hatte einen wichtigen Teil seines Ein-
kommens ausgemacht, und als dann, vor allem nach dem Zweiten
Weltkrieg, die Pferde ausblieben, schloß er 1957 seine Schmiede.

Weitere Veränderungen in der Erwerbsstruktur

Noch dramatischer als der Rückgang des landwirtschaftlichen
Bereichs ist der des Schnitzereiwesens. Gab es noch in den fünfziger
Jahren Werkstätten, in denen an die siebzig Leute arbeiteten, so
findet man dort heute nicht einmal mehr eine Handvoll Schnitzer.
Teilweise liegt das an einem Rückgang der Nachfrage nach religiöser
Kunst, teilweise vielleicht an einem Wandel des Kunstverständnisses,
teilweise aber sicherlich daran, daß wir, wie Walter Benjamin er-
kannte, „im Zeitalter der technischen Reproduktion" leben. In Ma-

egantly dressed theatergoers. Even though one can still get his milk from the farm fresh from the cow, the number of farms is greatly reduced, and with it the number of cows, and their presence in the village.

Even more decisive was the decline in transport by horse. For many centuries a good number of Oberammergauers had earned their living by offering their services with horse and wagon, which had to be driven from the Loisach valley over a steep climb to the Ammer valley, which lay 200 meters higher. And horses were abundantly employed in agriculture. Horses often pulled coaches or the so-called "Stellwagen," a sort of horse omnibus, which competed for quite some time with the modern motorized omnibus. My father, who came to Oberammergau in 1929, drove tourists from Oberammergau to the castle Lindhof in such a vehicle, and there's a handsome photograph of my father perched like a proud coachman on the box with my mother, who is sitting shyly next to him in her boarding-school uniform. In the 1930s, like many others, he gave up the horse and wagon and bought a modern motorized truck. My grandfather the blacksmith was also directly affected by such developments. Much of his income came from shoeing horses, and since there weren't many horses left, especially after World War II, he closed his shop in 1957.

Further Changes in the Nature of Work

More dramatic than the decline in agriculture is the decline in the woodcarving industry. Where in the 1950s there were once workshops where as many as seventy people worked, one can only find but a handful today. This is partly due to the decline in demand for religious art, partly to a change in the appreciation of art, and certainly also the fact that we live, as Walter Benjamin realized, "in the age of reproduction through technology." Materials such as plastic lend themselves more easily to technological reproduction, and thus plastic objects stripped wooden objects, which are much more labor-inten-

terialien wie Plastik läßt es sich leichter technisch reproduzieren, so daß daraus hergestellte Gegenstände denen aus dem Werkstoff Holz, der viel aufwendiger zu bearbeiten ist, auf dem Markt den Rang ablaufen. Der früher bedeutende Zweig der Spielzeugherstellung liegt daher z. B. völlig darnieder. Auch wuchs den handgefertigten Schnitzwaren Konkurrenz zu durch maschinell an Fräsen hergestellte Figuren, die ersteren zum Verwechseln ähnlich sehen. Durch derartige Billigwaren, massenhaft vor allem in Südtirol, mittlerweile aber auch in Fernost hergestellt, werden die handwerklichen Produkte verdrängt.

Die Oberammergauer Schnitzer reagieren auf diese Probleme, indem sie ganz individuelle Wege gehen. Der eine spezialisiert sich auf das Schnitzen von Tieren, der andere auf skurrile, um Eier herum aufgebaute Figuren, ein dritter—in Rückbesinnung auf die traditionellen Fadengaukler—auf surreale Hampelmänner, ein vierter auf Masken und ein anderer wieder auf anspruchsvolle Restaurierungsarbeiten. In den verschiedensten Stilrichtungen werden—auch von einer ganzen Reihe akademischer Bildhauer—qualitätvolle künstlerische Arbeiten hergestellt. Viele hochbegabte Schnitzer aber, die das Los einer niedrigen Bezahlung für eine hochqualifizierte Arbeit nicht mehr hinnehmen wollen, wechseln auch in andere Berufe.

An Bedeutung zugenommen hat sicher das Dienstleistungsgewerbe, vor allem wuchsen die vielerlei Bereiche, die mit dem Tourismus verbunden sind. Eine zunehmend wichtigere Rolle spielen außerdem Einrichtungen des Gesundheitswesens, z. B. ein deutschlandweit renommiertes Rheumazentrum und eine Rehabilitationsklinik. Oder auch Einrichtungen der Altenfürsorge wie große Altersheime. Angesichts des Rückgangs einiger traditioneller Gewerbe wie des notwendigen Verzichts auf Industrien, die die Natur und die Erholungsqualität des Ortes beeinträchtigen könnten, ist die Gemeinde interessiert an der Ansiedlung einer „sanften Industrie", und sie ist z. B. sehr froh darüber, wenn die Nato-Schule plant, ihre derzeitige Lehrgangskapazität von ca. 6000 Teilnehmern auf jährlich 12000 zu verdoppeln.

Was außerdem bleibt

Greatorex' Zeichnung „The Gathering of the Band" zeigt, wie die Blasmusik, damals „türkische Musik" genannt, zu spielen beginnt

sive to produce, of their position in the marketplace. The production of toys, for example, once an important business for the area, is now no fully depressed. Factory-produced figures competed further with hand-carved objects, and one often can't tell the difference between them. The hand-crafted products are being displaced by these cheap products, which are manufactured primarily in southern Tirol, but also in the Far East.

The woodcarvers of Oberammergau react to these problems by going their own individual ways. One specializes in carving animals; another in bizarre figures built around eggs; a third, finding inspiration in traditional toys with pull strings, makes surreal jumping jacks; a fourth makes masks; and yet another specializes in exacting restoration work. Quality artistic works are produced in a great variety of styles, also by an assortment of trained sculptors. But many talented woodcarvers, who'll no longer stand for being paid so little for such high-quality work, move to other careers.

The service sector has certainly gained in importance; above all the various services connected with tourism have grown. Also health establishments are playing an increasingly important role, examples being a rheumatic center known throughout Germany and a rehabilitation clinic, as well as establishments to care for the elderly, such as large nursing homes. In the face of the decline of some traditional trades, and of the necessary rejection of industries that could adversely affect the unspoiled environment and the salutary effects of the village, the community is interested in "soft industries" moving in. The town is very happy, for example, that the NATO school plans to double its course capacity, from about 6,000 annual participants to 12,000.

What Remains

Greatorex's drawing "The Gathering of the Band" shows the band starting to play wind music, then called "Turkish music," and big and small are lured to it. It's the moment when

und Groß und Klein heranlockt. Es handelt sich um den Moment,
wo nach einem den nahen Spielbeginn signalisierenden Böllerschuß
die Musikkapelle die Zuschauer um sich scharte, um sie dann mit
klingendem Spiel zum Theater zu geleiten. Hier tritt ein Element
zutage, das zentral ist für Oberammergau: die Musik. Bezeich-
nenderweise ist fast ein Drittel des Passionsspiels musikalisch ge-
staltet, wobei sowohl Rochus Dedler, der Komponist der Musik von
1811–20, aus Oberammergau stammte wie Eugen Papst, der Bearbeiter
von 1950, und Markus Zwink, der sie für 2000 erneut überarbeitete
und durch neue Nummern ergänzte. Daß es heute in dem 5000-
Einwohner-Ort drei große Chöre gibt, ein Symphonieorchester und
ein Blasmusikorchester, wo jeweils auf hohem Niveau gesungen und
musiziert wird, dazu viele kleinere Gruppen, die klassische Kammer-
musik, bayerische Tanzmusik, Jazz, Rock oder auch Klezmermusik
spielen, des weiteren kleinere Gesangsformationen, wo man von Re-
naissancemadrigalen bis Arvo Paert, von bayerischen Gstanzln bis zu
Comedian Harmonists-Nummern Stimmiges und Eindrucksvolles zu
hören bekommt,—all das beweist, daß in Oberammergau die Musik-
tradition lebt. Welche übergeordnete Bedeutung die Musik hat, das
kommt auch zum Ausdruck in einem Deckengemälde der Pfarrkirche, das den Himmel als den Ort imaginiert, wo singend, gei-
gend, flötend miteinander kommuniziert und konzertiert wird.

Die Freude an der Geselligkeit, wie sie sich mit der Musik
verbinden kann—auch sie ist ein bleibendes Element des dörflichen
Lebens. Allegria, heiter schwebende, leichte Fröhlichkeit, kann man
hier fast wie in Italien finden, in besonders schöner Ausprägung
nach Theaterpremieren, die hier nicht selten zu erleben sind. Und
auch das, die Lust am Theaterspielen,— nicht nur im Passionsspiel, sondern mit Shakespeare-Stücken oder Bauerntheater,—
gehört zu den Bereichen mit Kontinuität.

Wollte man für Musik und Theaterspielen die Formel
akzeptieren „Sensibilität plus Vitalität plus X“, so wäre diese Formel
auch brauchbar für eine Tätigkeit, die hier gerade unter jungen Leuten
sehr verbreitet ist: Bergwandern und Bergsteigen bzw. Klettern. Denn
hier geht es nicht nur um eine Sportart, die Mut, Kraft und Geschick
fordert. Wenngleich man dadurch ein wenig die Welt zum Sportgerät

the band gathers the audience together after a small cannon signals the imminent beginning of the play; the guests are then led to the theater to harmonious strains. This brings a central element for Oberammergau to light: music. Significantly, almost one-third of the Passion Play is set to music. Creators of this music, all from Oberammergau, are Rochus Dedler, music composer from 1811 to 1820, as well as Eugen Papst, arranger from 1950, and Markus Zwink, who reworked the music for 2000 and added new numbers. The fact that in this 5,000-resident village there are three large choirs, a symphony orchestra, and a woodwind orchestra, all meeting high performance standards; many small groups that play classical chamber music, Bavarian dance music, jazz, rock, and even Klezmer music; and even smaller groups with upbeat and impressive offerings, everything from Renaissance madrigals to Arvo Paert, from Bavarian folk songs to Comedian Harmonists numbers—all of this proves that the tradition of music is alive and well in Oberammergau. The great significance that music has is expressed on a ceiling fresco in the parish church; it depicts heaven as a place where there is singing and violin and flute playing, where concertizing and communion are one.

The pleasure in sociability, as it can be found in music, is a sustained element of village life. *Allegria*, a cheerful, lilting, and simple happiness, can be experienced here, almost like in Italy, in especially fine form after theater premiers, which are not rare here. Joy in the theater—not just the Passion Play, but also Shakespeare's plays or peasant farces—is a continuing experience.

If one accepts the equation for theater and music "sensitivity + vitality + x," it is also appropriate for an activity that is currently very widespread among the youth: hiking and mountain and rock climbing. These aren't just sports that demand courage, strength, and skill. Even though this sort of turns the world into a piece of sports equipment, still there is an attitude that in old-fashioned terms could be consid-

macht, so verbindet sich damit doch meist auch eine Haltung, die man
altmodisch als Schöpfungsfrömmigkeit bezeichnen könnte, eine
fundamentale, mehr oder weniger religiös gefärbte Dankbarkeit dafür,
daß da ist, was da ist, auch dafür, daß die Welt schön ist.

Natürlich tradieren sich bei den Oberammergauern manche
weitere Eigenschaften, die hier nicht alle ausgebreitet werden
können. Angesprochen werden muß aber die Liebe zur Tradition,
wobei diese durchaus ganz unideologisch sein kann. Erleben kann
man sie etwa am 24. August, bei der jährlichen Erinnerungsfeier
für Ludwig II., bei der prächtigen Fronleichnams-Prozession mit
bunten Trachten, wehenden Fahnen und blumengeschmückten
Altären oder beim „Sterngang" am Silvesterabend, wenn die Bevölkerung, einem beleuchteten Stern mit einer Darstellung des
Christus-Kinds folgend, durch den Ort zieht. Und natürlich bestimmt diese Liebe zur Tradition auch das nunmehr zum 40. Mal
seit 1634 aufgeführte Passionsspiel.

Tradition und Offenheit für das Leben—ein Widerspruch?

Nun gibt es ja Spielarten der Traditionsgebundenheit, die nicht un-
problematisch sind. Nicht selten verbindet sich mit dem Wunsch, an
einer überkommenen Lebensform oder Weltanschauung festzuhalten,
eine Abwehr des Heute, eine bis zum Paranoiden gehende Angst, die
eigene Identität sei bedroht. Sie kann nach außen hin zu Aggressivität,
nach innen hin zu Erstarrung führen—wofür leider nicht nur der Iran
ein Beispiel ist. Im Rückblick auf die Rezeptionsgeschichte des
Oberammergauer Passionsspiels läßt sich erkennen, daß seit dem 19.
Jahrhundert konservativ bis fundamentalistisch orientierte Gruppen,
die von derartigen Gefährdungen nicht frei waren, Oberammergau,
das seit Jahrhunderten gegen alle Widerstände sein Passionsspiel
behauptet hatte, zu ihrem Symbol deklarierten. Sie und andere ver-
suchten immer wieder Oberammergau ideologisch zu vereinnahmen.
So auch die Nationalsozialisten, die die Passion als „bäuerliches Spiel"
aus der „segnenden Kraft der Scholle" interpretierten, woraus man
die Lehre ziehen sollte, „daß die Treue zu Blut und Boden die Haltkraft
allen Volkstums" sei.

Von derartigen Angeboten der Interpretation seiner selbst

ered piety toward creation, a fundamental, more or less religiously colored thankfulness for that fact that what is there is
there and also that the world is so beautiful.

Naturally, there are many other traditional characteristics in Oberammergau that cannot be detailed here. Their
love of tradition, often not at all connected to ideologies,
should, however, be addressed. One can experience tradition
on August 24 at the annual remembrance celebration for
Ludwig II, at the splendid Corpus Christi procession with
colorful dresses, waving flags, and altars decorated with flowers, or at the star-lantern procession on New Year's Eve, when
the townspeople follow a lighted star with an image of the
Christ Child through the village. And this love of tradition is
naturally what accounts for the Passion Play, which has been
shown forty times since 1634.

Tradition and Openness in Life—a Contradiction?

There are varieties of tradition-keeping that are not without
problems. Often the desire to hold on to a traditional lifestyle
or worldview combines with an aversion to the present, a fear
that escalates to paranoia of one's identity being threatened.
This can lead to outward aggression or inner paralysis, for
which Iran is unfortunately but one example. Looking in retrospect at the history of the Oberammergau Passion Play's
reception, one can see that since the nineteenth century, there
have been conservative and fundamentalist groups that were
not free from these dangers. These groups claimed as their
symbol Oberammergau, which for centuries had defended its
Passion Play against all sorts of opposition, and they continually tried to co-opt Oberammergau ideologically. Thus the
National Socialists pronounced the Passion Play to be a "rustic
play," stemming from the "sacred power of the motherland,"
from which one should draw the lesson "that loyalty to blood
and soil [is] the sustaining power of a people."

Oberammergau must continually free itself from

muß Oberammergau sich immer wieder freimachen. Und sogar wenn
die Namen „Oberammergau" und „Passionsspiel" fast zu Synonymen
für „Tradition" geworden sind, kann sich der Ort nicht völlig auf
eine solche Rolle fixieren lassen. Keine Gesellschaft, auch Oberammergau nicht, kann sich absolut nur im Tradierten einrichten und
von aller Entwicklung abkoppeln. Auch wenn man angesichts einer
sich in immer kürzeren Zyklen verändernden Welt die Sehnsucht nach
der Welt von Gestern, nach einer stabilen, vertrauten Ordnung
verstehen kann. Doch wie der Eiserne Vorhang den Osten gegenüber
den Entwicklungen des Westens nicht abschotten konnte und schließlich angesichts moderner Informationsübertragung per Satellit zu
einem absurden Zeugnis eines Dogmatismus wurde, wäre es sinnlos,
Oberammergau als Museum unter eine Glasglocke stellen zu wollen.
     Auch hier dröhnt einem z. B. aus dem Radio des Last-
wagens, mit dem das altvertraute bayerische Nationalgetränk Bier
ins Haus geliefert wird, internationale Popmusik entgegen. Auch
der vorliegende Essay ist auf einem Computer geschrieben und wird
per e-mail versandt werden, so daß er in New York oder Lafayette
schneller aus dem Internet geholt werden kann, als ich den Ausdruck davon zu meinem Oberammergauer Nachbarn bringen
könnte. Allerdings wird dann der gleiche Bierlieferant, wenn er die
Rechnung bringt, sie in bayerischem Dialekt kommentieren. Oder
er setzt sich, wie jahrelang der Bierlieferant meiner Eltern, ein wenig
zur Familie und trinkt einen Café und erzählt ein wenig, Lustiges
oder Ernstes, und da er auch der Organist der Pfarrkirche ist, sam-
meln sich bei ihm Informationen über das Leben im Dorf, besonders weil er am Sonntag mit den zahlreichen Chorsängern und
Orchestermusikern zusammenkommt, wenn sie die Orchestermessen
eines Haydn oder Mozart oder des Komponisten der Passionsmusik
Rochus Dedler spielen. Schon das Beispiel zeigt, wie Modernes und
Überkommenes ineinander übergehen. Es läßt auch ahnen, daß es bei
allen Veränderungen des Alltags durch Technik, neue Medien etc. doch
starke Kontinuitäten im mentalen Bereich gibt. Ganz wesentlich auch
in der Art des zwischenmenschlichen Umgangs.
     Allerdings darf eine klare Zäsur nicht außer Acht gelassen
werden, die Oberammergau betrifft als einen Ort in Deutschland: die

such interpretations. Even though the name "Oberammergau" and "Passion Play" have practically become synonymous with "tradition," the village cannot allow itself to be bound to such a role. No society, Oberammergau included, can isolate itself from all change and fix itself absolutely in traditions. In view of the current world, with its waves of change coming in ever shorter cycles, one can understand the longing for yesterday's world, a world of stable, familiar order. But just as the Iron Curtain could not seal the East off from Western developments and finally, in the face of modern information transfer by satellite, became an absurd testament to dogmatism, so would it be senseless to want to keep Oberammergau in a bubble and turn it into a museum.

Here also, there's international pop music, for example, booming out of the radio in the truck that delivers the dearly loved Bavarian national beverage, beer, to my house. This essay was written on a computer and will be sent via email, so that it can be downloaded in New York or Lafayette faster than I can take a copy of it to my neighbor in Oberammergau. The same beer deliverer will, of course, speak Bavarian dialect when he brings the bill, and maybe he'll sit with the family, like the delivery man of my parents' time, have a cup of coffee, and talk a bit, about some funny or serious topic. And because he's also the organist in the parish church, he is a compendium of information about life in the village, especially because he gets together with the numerous choir singers and orchestra players on Sunday when they play the masses of Haydn, Mozart, or the Passion Play composer, Rochus Dedler. This particular example shows how the modern and the traditional overlap. It also suggests that even with all the changes that come about through technology, new media, etc., there are still strong continuities in how we think. These continuities are intrinsic in the way people relate to one another.

We cannot disregard a clear turning point that affected Oberammergau as a German village: that separating the

zwischen der Zeit bis 1945 und der darauf folgenden Zeit. Das be-
schämende Entdecken des während nationalsozialistischer Herrschaft
Geschehenen, die Diskussionen über die Gründe und Zusammen-
hänge, aus denen Inhumanität erwachsen konnte, das Erlernen von
Bürgerselbstbewußtsein und demokratischer Auseinandersetzung (auch
seitens hierarchiegewohnter Katholiken), die schmerzhaften Streitig-
keiten zwischen den Generationen, die Verbreitung aktueller Einsichten
durch ein modernes Schulsystem wie durch die Medien, die Begegnung
mit immer neuen, ob aus Frankreich, ob aus Amerika kommenden
Ideen über eine Verbesserung der Welt oder die Entfaltung der in-
dividuellen Möglichkeiten, die Auseinandersetzung mit politischen,
religiösen, psychologischen Vorstellungen, die auch durch Studierende
oder in der Welt herumkommende Oberammergauer teils befruchtend,
teils verwirrend in das Dorf hereingetragen wurden,—all das führte
letztlich nach 1945 doch zu großen mentalen Veränderungen.

Vor allem zu einer größeren Offenheit—selbst wenn es
auch schon früher eine „Liberalitas Bavarica" gab und die Devise
„Leben und leben lassen" vielfach den Umgang miteinander bestimmt hatte. Waren nicht schon die Klöster ringsum, die z. B. vor
1800 ganz optimistisch die Ideen der französischen Aufklärung auf-
nahmen, Orte größter geistiger Offenheit gewesen? Mit einer
solchen Einstellung kann sich durchaus Traditionsbewußtsein verbinden, in dem Sinn, daß das Wissen um die Vielfalt früherer Zeiten
zu Gelassenheit gegenüber der Gegenwart führt—gepaart mit
einem Schuß Skeptizismus gegenüber allem aufgeregt Modernen.

Das Ringen um die rechte Weise des Tradierens

Eine Tradition weiterzugeben, bedeutet, nach einem französischen
Bonmot, das Feuer, nicht die Asche weiterzugeben. Das gilt besonders für das Passionsspiel, das nun seit erstaunlichen 366 Jahren
tradiert worden ist. Immer wieder galt und gilt es, die
nachwachsende Generation für die überkommene Aufgabe zu be-
geistern. Und immer wieder steht Oberammergau vor der Aufgabe,
den richtigen Weg des Tradierens zu finden.

Gerade bei einem Passionsspiel kann es ja nicht nur um
die Weitergabe einer Form gehen, auch nicht, wenn man—wie mehr-

pre-1945 period from the subsequent period. The shaming discovery of the actions during the Nazi rule, the discussions over the reasons and contexts from which this inhumanity could grow, the learning of consciousness as a citizenry and of democratic debate (especially among the Catholics, who are used to hierarchies), the painful arguments between the generations, the dissemination of crucial views through a modern school system as well as through the media, the encounter with new ideas, whether from France or American, on how to improve the world or develop individual potentials, the debate with political, religious, and psychological notions that were brought into Oberammergau, some by students, some by citizens who had traveled abroad, some bearing fruit and some resulting in confusion—all this led to great changes in our way of thinking after 1945.

It led above all to a great openness—even though a "Liberalitas Bavarica" already existed earlier, and the motto "live and let live" had in many ways determined relations. Weren't the monasteries all around, which, for example, optimistically adopted the ideas of the French Enlightenment before 1800, places of great intellectual openness? A consciousness of tradition can coexist with this attitude of openness, in the sense that knowledge of the diversity of past ages leads to composure toward the present—paired with a shot of skepticism toward the frantic modern age.

Struggling for the Right Way to Pass on Tradition

To pass on a tradition, according to a French witticism, means to pass on the fire, not the ashes. This is especially true for the Passion Play, which has been tradition for an amazing 366 years. It has always been, and still is, a question of developing enthusiasm for the inherited duty among the younger generation, and Oberammergau continually faces the task of finding the right way to pass on the tradition.

Especially in the case of a passion play, it's not just a question of passing on a form, even though it seems—

fach im Lauf der Oberammergauer Spielgeschichte—eine der
Komplexität und der Bedeutung der Inhalte angemessene, ästhetisch
überzeugende Form gefunden zu haben schien. Auch wenn eine
Gestaltung akzeptiert, kanonisiert, sozusagen klassisch geworden
war, hat man sich davon wieder und wieder gelöst. In jedem Bereich,
hinsichtlich des Textes wie der Bilder. Mit der Kontinuität verband
sich in Oberammergau—wenngleich es Phasen der Stagnation gab
—ein Element der Erneuerung.

Dafür gab es zwei Impulse. Erstens ist die Geschichte Jesu,
seines Engagements, das den Widerstand gegen ihn provozierte,
seines Endes bzw. gerade seines Nicht-Endes, eine rätselhafte und
geheimnisvolle Geschichte, die Grundfragen des Lebens aufrührt.
Keine Generation kann umhin, sie jeweils neu zu dechiffrieren, ihre
Bedeutung und Kraft zu entdecken, die—wie die Entstehung des
Spiels zeigt—so groß ist, daß man dadurch aus der Herrschaft
des Todes zum Leben findet. Letztlich gilt es, die Gestalt zu suchen,
die im Zentrum des Spiels steht.

Zweitens ist die Geschichte in einem immer wieder ver-
änderten historischen Kontext zu erzählen, einem sich verändernden Publikum durch sich verändernde Spieler. Da Wörter, Bilder,
auch die musikalische Gestalt—alles Formale dem Wandel der
Zeiten unterworfen ist, gilt es immer erneut die ästhetischen Mittel
zu finden, mit denen die Geschichte erzählt werden kann. In einer
Weise, daß sie die Zuschauer erreicht und die ihr innewohnende
Kraft entfaltet, dabei auch nicht verkleinert, ideologisiert, verfälscht
wird. Im Grunde geht es um eine immer erneute Inkulturisation
der „Christusenergie"— wie der Künstler Beus diese Kraft nannte.

Ähnlich wie es eine fortlaufende Auseinandersetzung
unter den Theologen um ein angemessenes Reden von Gott und
seinem Sohn gibt und unter Künstlern eine nie zu beendende Diskussion über einen wahrhaftigen Ausdruck des Religiösen, so gehört auch zu Oberammergau die Auseinandersetzung—mit allem,
was dies an sozialen und politischen Konflikten bedeutet. Aber nur,
wenn diese Suche vorausgeht, besteht die Möglichkeit, daß der
Besucher, wie er es erhofft, in Oberammergau Authentisches findet.
So kam es auch auf das Jahr 2000 hin erst durch einen langwierigen

as is repeatedly shown in the history of the Oberammergau play—that an aesthetically persuasive form had been
found that was commensurate with the complexity and weight
of the play's subject matter. Even when a form has been accepted, canonized, and has so to speak become a classic, one
deviates from it again and again, in every area, textual and
visual. In Oberammergau, an element of renewal—even
though there were phases of stagnation—associates itself with
the continuity.

There were two impulses for this. First, the story of
Jesus, his commitment, which provoked resistance to him, his
end, leading to his immortality, a mysterious and puzzling
story, brings up life's fundamental questions. No generation
can help deciphering the story anew, discovering its meaning
and power, which, as the origin of the play shows, are so immense, that one escapes death's reign and attain life. Ultimately,
it is about finding the character that's central to the play.

Secondly, the story is told in a constantly changing
historical context to a changing audience and by changing per-
formers. Because words, images, and musical forms—that is,
all formal aspects—are subject to changing times, it is always
necessary to find the aesthetic means to tell the story. A way
must be found that reaches the audience and that unfolds the
story's inner power, but at the same time doesn't trivialize, ide-
ologize, or falsify. The basic issue is one of the renewed
enculturation of the "Christ energy," as the artist Beus called
this power.

Just as there is a continued debate among theologians
about a suitable discussion of God and His Son, and among
artists a never-ending discussion about true expression of the
religious, so Oberammergau has its debate—with all of the
social and political conflicts it entails. But only with seeking
does the possibility arise for the visitor to find authenticity in
Oberammergau, as he had hoped. So in the year 2000 as well,
it was only through a lengthy process of public discussion that
it was decided to rework the text and music, create new sets

Prozeß der öffentlichen Diskussion dazu, daß Text und Musik umfassend bearbeitet, neue Bühnenbilder und Kostüme geschaffen werden konnten, und man dann versuchen konnte, in zahllosen Proben den Gestalten auf die Spur zu kommen.

Einen Maßstab zur Beurteilung der Frage, wie man es mit dem Tradieren halten solle, gibt sogar die Passionsgeschichte selbst. Denn diesem Drama liegt wesentlich der Konflikt zu Grunde, daß zwar Jesus wie seine Gegner aus der religiösen Szene den Anspruch erheben, die Tradition Israels weiterzuführen, daß aber die Frage, wie sie weiterzuführen sei, kontrovers beantwortet wird. Die Antwort des historischen Jesus scheint die absolute Bindung des Herzens an Gott und den Nächsten gewesen zu sein.

Auch wenn sich ein Spiel so nahe an den Rand des Geheimnisses wagt, so kann es doch nur bescheiden in die Richtung des Geheimnisses weisen, es nur ansagen, doch es darf nicht den Anspruch erheben, es zur Gänze auszusagen. Unser Unterfangen ist begrenzt. Aber auch das Wissen um solche Begrenztheit kann man als eine Oberammergauer Tradition sehen. Es kommt z. B. zum Ausdruck in einem Duett am Beginn des Spiels, dessen Worte im Jahr 2000 genauso wieder zu hören sein werden, wie sie es 1871 waren, als Eliza Greatorex die Passionsspiele besuchte:

> Ew'ger, höre Deiner Kinder Stammeln,
> da ein Kind ja nichts als stammeln kann . . .

and costumes, and then through countless rehearsals to try to capture the essence of the characters.

The passion story itself presents a yardstick for judging the question of how one should carry on tradition. This drama is essentially based on the conflict in which Jesus and his adversaries both lay claim to the determination of how the tradition of Israel should be carried on; but this question ends up being answered in a controversial way. The answer from the historical Jesus appears to have been an absolute binding of one's heart to God and to one's neighbor.

Even when a play ventures so close to the edge of a mystery, it can really only modestly point in the direction of the mystery; only intimate it, never dare to spell it out in its entirety. Our venture is limited. But one can see this knowledge of our limits as an Oberammergau tradition. It is expressed, for example, in a duet at the beginning of the play, whose words can be understood in the year 2000 just as they were understood in 1871 when Eliza Greatorex visited the Passion Play:

> Eternal One, hear your children stammer,
> as a child can do no more than stammer. . .